Reimagining the Mathematics Classroom

Creating and Sustaining Productive Learning Environments, K–Grade 6

By

Cathery Yeh
Chapman University
Orange, California

Mark W. Ellis
California State University, Fullerton
Fullerton, California

Carolee Koehn Hurtado
University of California, Los Angeles
Los Angeles, California

NATIONAL COUNCIL OF
TEACHERS OF MATHEMATICS

www.nctm.org/more4u
Access code: RSC15000

Copyright © 2017 by
The National Council of Teachers of Mathematics, Inc.
1906 Association Drive, Reston, VA 20191-1502
(703) 620-9840; (800) 235-7566; www.nctm.org
All rights reserved
Sixth Printing

Library of Congress Cataloging-in-Publication Data

Names: Yeh, Cathery. | Ellis, Mark W. (Mark William), 1969- | Hurtado, Carolee Koehn, 1976-

Title: Reimagining the mathematics classroom : creating and sustaining productive learning
    environments, K–6 / by Cathery Yeh, Chapman University, Orange, California,
    Mark W. Ellis, California State University, Fullerton, Fullerton, California,
    Carolee Koehn Hurtado, University of California, Los Angeles.

Description: Reston, VA : The National Council of Teachers of Mathematics, [2016]

Identifiers: LCCN 2016021513 (print) | LCCN 2016030152 (ebook) | ISBN 9780873539081
    (pbk.) | ISBN 9780873539012 (ebook)

Subjects: LCSH: Mathematics—Study and teaching (Elementary) | School improvement programs.

Classification: LCC QA135.6 .Y44 2016 (print) | LCC QA135.6 (ebook) | DDC 372.7-dc23

LC record available at https://lccn.loc.gov/2016021513

The National Council of Teachers of Mathematics advocates for high-quality
mathematics teaching and learning for each and every student.

Printed in the United States of America

Contents

Acknowledgments

We have had the good fortune to work with a number of generous and thoughtful colleagues who have helped shape our thinking and who continue to inspire our work. Our utmost thanks and appreciation go to the teachers whose classrooms, practices, and students are featured throughout this book. Their daily efforts bring to life the research and theories about instructional practices that best serve all learners in making sense of mathematics. Their dedication and exemplary work make our work possible and bring the greatest value to the ideas within these pages. These teachers' names appear at the end of this section.

We also want to thank NCTM's Educational Materials Committee reviewers whose comments and critical insights provided focus to our early efforts. And we thank the following outside reviewers whose feedback on our near-final drafts shaped the final product: Robert Berry, Jody Guarino, Megan Holmstrom, Jennifer Lawyer, Alicia Lloyd, Bethany Lockhart, Karen Recinos, Theodore Sagun, Rosa Serratore, Juanita Walker, and Janene Ward.

Finally, we could not have done this without the love and support of our families. They encouraged us to take on the challenge of writing this book, marshaling the support and patience needed when a spouse or mom says, "Just one more minute while I finish this sentence," and then finally pushes away from the computer hours later. Thank you for hanging in there with us and understanding how much this project means to us.

Teachers Featured in This Book

Jenny Kim Bae, Waite Middle School, Norwalk, California

Christine Bouma, Crane Country Day School, Santa Barbara, California

Jean Chen-Wu, A. E. Arnold Elementary School, Cypress, California

Holly Compton, Pacific Elementary School, Manhattan Beach, California

Vanessa Frank, McGaugh Elementary School, Seal Beach, California

Ruth Freedman-Finch, Weaver Elementary School, Los Alamitos, California

Brett Geithman, Manhattan Beach Unified School District, Manhattan Beach, California

Lauren Guite, Viejo Elementary School, Mission Viejo, California

Vanessa Hayward, William Green Elementary School, Lawndale, California

Cherise Jones, Mark Twain Elementary School, Lawndale, California

Heidi Kwalk, Weaver Elementary School, Los Alamitos, California

Jennifer Lawyer, William Green Elementary School, Lawndale, California

Alicia Lloyd, William Green and Billy Mitchell Elementary Schools, Lawndale, California

Teri Malpass, Oak Middle School, Los Alamitos, California

Desiree Olivas, Garfield Elementary School, Santa Ana, California

Mayra Orozco, Adelaide Price Elementary School, Anaheim, California

Kelley Otani, Weaver Elementary School, Los Alamitos, California

Jenny Padilla, William Green Elementary School, Lawndale, California

Jean Pryor, John Burroughs Middle School, Los Angeles, California

David Rhodes, Lathrop Intermediate School, Santa Ana, California

Lisa So, Weaver Elementary School, Los Alamitos, California

Marie Sykes, Chaparral Elementary School, Ladera Ranch, California

Darielle Tom, Weaver Elementary School, Los Alamitos, California

Introduction

In this book, we focus on students' learning of powerful mathematics. We use the term "powerful" in our description of mathematics for several reasons. First of all, mathematics carries particular power in our society; success in mathematics is critical for academic success. More than any other subject, mathematics affects students' college and career opportunities. The highest high school mathematics class for which a student earns credit has a major influence on college acceptance and college graduation (Lee 2012). However, while mathematics success is significant for college and career success, by the time students reach middle school, the majority think it is too boring or too hard, with over half expressing both a lack of interest and a dislike for the subject (Mullis et al. 2012; U.S. Department of Education 2014). In addition, U.S. students in the early elementary school years learn to associate mathematics success with speed and accuracy (Boaler 2015), rather than with reasoning and sense making. Being good at mathematics comes to be seen as a talent or skill one is born with: some may be born mathematically gifted, while others are not (Boaler 2015). But this is simply not true!

We have written this book with the goal of challenging narrow conceptions of mathematics learning and mathematics achievement. Decades of research, as well as the work of the teachers and students highlighted in this book, demonstrate that mathematical success can and should be available for all. This body of work makes clear that each student's success in mathematics is greatly influenced by the opportunities and support for learning provided by teachers. *Principles to Actions* (NCTM 2014a) calls for schools and classrooms to shift from "pockets of excellence" to "systemic excellence" where every aspect of our instruction is carefully considered to maximize student learning. Thinking about the learning environment as a system is important because all facets of instructional decision making—the classroom layout, the opportunity for student talk, the tasks assigned, the assessments used, the availability and use of technology and tools, and the involvement of families and communities—affect student learning and convey to students what is valued and who is valued in the classroom.

Three principles guide our discussion of creating productive, inclusive mathematics learning environments:

1. Teach toward the understanding of powerful mathematics.
2. View students as sense makers with valuable, important ideas.
3. Nurture a mathematics community of learners.

These principles are at the heart of creating classrooms where children can participate meaningfully and equitably with mathematics and with each other. The challenge, of course, lies in putting these principles into practice, which is what we hope this book will support teachers in doing. The classroom vignettes in this book reflect insights we have gained about designing productive mathematics learning environments from working closely with and learning from teachers who are committed to equity in student learning opportunities and outcomes. These vignettes are inspired by the ways these learning environments have been designed to support teacher and student practices that demonstrate the transformative potential within student-centered instruction. Just as these teachers have inspired us, we hope their everyday practices will illuminate possibilities for other teachers seeking to create classrooms that disrupt long-standing assumptions about what it means to know and understand mathematics and who can and cannot excel in mathematics.

We'll now talk a bit more about each of these principles and then provide an outline of what lies ahead in the rest of the book.

Principle 1: Teach Toward the Understanding of Powerful Mathematics

The building of powerful mathematics starts from understanding. What is understanding of mathematics? Our conception of mathematical understanding is rooted in a notion of proficiency as knowing more than isolated facts and methods. It requires "an integrated and functional grasp of mathematical ideas . . . which enables students to learn new ideas by connecting those ideas to what they already know" (National Research Council [NRC] 2001, p. 118). Knowledge that is learned with understanding is rich in connections and is generative, helping to support further learning. To develop learning with understanding requires that teachers know strategies to connect new knowledge with students' prior knowledge and know which connections are most productive in supporting students' problem solving and future mathematics learning.

This view of mathematical understanding requires approaching learning as building from students' existing knowledge, posing questions that provoke curiosity, and supporting students in developing habits of mathematical reasoning and sense making. Through habits, or practices, of reasoning, children begin to make connections between rules, procedures, and concepts. They come to see coherence among mathematical ideas, recognize a purpose for mathematics in their lives, and maybe even discover pleasure in exploring mathematics. This book will share strategies for planning and implementing tasks to support such learning.

Principle 2: View Students as Sense Makers with Valuable, Important Ideas

Mathematical knowledge and understanding cannot be transferred directly from teacher to student. Students must be provided with opportunities to construct their own knowledge and understanding in ways that reflect, refine, and extend their prior knowledge, skills, and experiences.

All children come to class with a great deal of practical mathematical knowledge and reasoning skills from their lived experiences. Students' existing knowledge and intuitive strategies for solving problems should be the basis for further learning. For example, kindergarten students without prior schooling have some intuitive knowledge of fractions from their experiences with fair sharing (e.g., sharing half a cookie with a sibling is about making two parts that are equal in size) but may not know that one-half can take on different shapes while remaining equivalent (e.g., cutting a square diagonally versus horizontally) or that whether one-half is more than one-third depends on whether they share a common whole. Students' rich experiences with mathematics, formal and informal, should serve as a starting point for building additional mathematical knowledge.

This leads us to realize that teachers must intentionally choose or design tasks that (a) reflect a deep understanding of mathematics as well as a deep understanding of those learning mathematics, and (b) promote and elicit students' thinking with and about mathematics. When these tasks are implemented, teachers must use instructional strategies that help students see mathematics as part of themselves and see themselves as owners and users of mathematics.

Principle 3: Nurture a Mathematics Community of Learners

> A community approach enhances learning: It helps to advance understanding, expand students' capabilities for investigation, enrich the questions that guide inquiry, and aid students in giving meaning to experiences. (NRC 1996, p. 46)

Learning for understanding is not an isolated or passive activity. It is above all a process of sense making and establishing meaning, both individually and collectively. Nurturing a learning community with the shared purpose of making sense of mathematics is vital to learning powerful mathematics.

We view a mathematics community of learners as an ecological system. In an ecosystem, such as a wetland or a desert, all aspects of life are interrelated and depend on each other's well-being. Teaching and learning are also built on relationships and interdependence. Students learn with and from each other in interaction with teachers and other adults in their lives. This book will highlight collaboration across varied activity structures—opportunities for students to work independently, in teams and small groups, and as a whole class—as well as within and beyond the classroom, a space that provides opportunities for every student to actively participate and to persevere in learning powerful mathematics. This sort of learning community must be intentionally created and nurtured, and it relies on clear and inclusive routines for participation so that societal inequities are not mirrored in the distribution of learning outcomes.

A Note about Tools and Technology

> An excellent mathematics program integrates the use of mathematical tools and technology as essential resources to help students learn and make sense of mathematical ideas, reason mathematically, and communicate their mathematical thinking. (NCTM 2014a, p. 78)

Tools (e.g., manipulatives, rulers, physical models) and technology (e.g., interactive whiteboards, computing devices, tablets) are resources that can help teachers and students enact the three principles to support powerful mathematics learning. In our view, it is not a question of whether to use tools and technology but how to use them to connect students to mathematics in ways that enable them to develop their own sense of ownership of mathematics. For this reason, we have integrated examples of tools and technology throughout each chapter. Look for text boxes that highlight specific-use cases of a particular tool or technology. At the end of the book, we also provide an annotated list of the tools and technology that are mentioned in the text.

How to Use This Book

This book is intended to help you, the educator, design a learning environment that engages students individually and collectively in meaningful learning experiences that promote sense making of mathematical ideas and mathematical reasoning. Each chapter describes one aspect of the learning environment by synthesizing the research and providing practical strategies that teachers can apply directly to their work.

Chapter 1 describes the physical attributes of the learning environment—the classroom layout, the wall space, and storage of manipulatives—as well as the use of virtual spaces to encourage teachers' and students' collaborative engagement with mathematics. Chapter 2 highlights the centrality of discourse and provides specific strategies, norms, and routines to support student discourse and promote equitable participation. Chapter 3 unpacks the characteristics of a rich mathematical task and offers guidance on how to carefully plan and enact lessons to allow and support students' productive engagement and perseverance. Chapter 4 examines the importance of assessment in supporting powerful learning and provides ideas on formative assessments that measure students' mathematical knowledge (conceptual, procedural, factual/notational) and mathematical practices (e.g., reasoning, justification, problem solving). Chapter 5 describes best practices and concrete examples of strategies to promote and strengthen home-school-community partnerships that support students' success with mathematics. Chapter 6 illustrates how these five elements come together in practice with vignettes of classroom teachers who are working to create learning environments that promote powerful mathematics for every student.

Each chapter contains the following features, either in the book itself or online at NCTM's More4U website:

- A synthesis of research applied to specific topics of this dimension of the learning environment, with concrete examples of how teachers have applied the concepts in their classrooms

- Video and classroom examples that offer a close look at how real teachers use the strategies from the chapter to teach mathematical concepts. Interviews with both students and teachers provide interesting insights on the rationale and outcome of specific teaching strategies.

- Handouts and materials for next-day use

Materials that are available online at More4U are listed in Appendix B, and readers may gain access to them by going to www.nctm.org/more4u and entering the access code located on the title page of this book.

It is our intention that this book portray ideas and images that reimagine the mathematics classroom as a place of possibility and powerful learning for all students, challenging what are often taken-for-granted beliefs and habits of mathematics teaching and learning that constrain opportunities to learn. While the way in which we have organized and described this content is ours, the research and practitioner knowledge and experiences that informed it come from a large community of mathematics educators—classroom teachers, school district administrators, engaged families, and university faculty—with a shared commitment to promoting powerful mathematics learning for all students. As you read through these pages and explore the digital resources at More4U, we hope you find support for both your efforts to make instructional shifts that support deeper learning in mathematics and your professional growth as a teacher of mathematics. And as you put some of these ideas into practice, we hope you find joy, as we have, in students' enthusiasm for making sense of mathematics, individually and collectively.

Finally, we want to acknowledge that the vision for mathematics teaching and learning we articulate requires collaboration among teachers, administrators, and families to have maximum impact, and that, in the process of working toward this goal, there will be lessons learned that inform us all about how to successfully engage in this work. We look forward to learning with and from these efforts and thank you in advance for sharing with us your successes and challenges along the way! Our understanding of putting research into practice is continually enriched and refined by what we learn from the passionate, committed teachers who on a daily basis create and nurture mathematics learning environments that support all students.

Chapter 1

The Physical and Virtual Environment

> Imagine a [learning environment] . . . where all students have access to high quality, engaging mathematics instruction. . . . The curriculum is mathematically rich, offering students opportunities to learn important mathematical concepts and procedures with understanding. . . . Alone or in groups and with access to [tools and] technology, they work productively and reflectively, with the skilled guidance of their teachers. Orally and in writing, students communicate their ideas and results effectively. They value mathematics and engage actively in learning it.
>
> —National Council of Teachers of Mathematics (NCTM),
> *Principles and Standards for School Mathematics*

Open the door to any classroom and you enter a unique space, the home away from home for teachers and their students. Teachers spend quite a lot of time on their classrooms—debating over the desk arrangements, deciding what should go on the walls, and designing places to store learning resources—and rightfully so because a classroom is not just a room. It is an environment. Just as the conditions of a natural environment affect whether species flourish or decline, the classroom's physical environment influences the learning that takes place there (Arndt 2012; Cheryan et al. 2014; S. Martin 2002; Marx, Fuhrer, and Hartig 1999; McGregor 2004). It all begins with how we design and make use of the physical space.

The physical environment sets the tone for students' first experiences with what it means to be a thinker and learner in our classrooms. Looking at space is about more than the visible structures; it is about the social relationships that are possible and what is communicated about expectations and participation structures for learning (McGregor 2004). What counts as learning and doing mathematics? And who can learn mathematics and be recognized as successful? If teachers want all students to have access to learning powerful mathematical ideas and to see themselves as mathematical thinkers and as scholars who collaboratively support one another's success, classroom spaces must be organized and utilized in ways that reflect and promote this vision.

A Peek Inside a Classroom

So, how do these principles come together in the design of the physical setting? Let's consider an example by looking into Marie Sykes's second-grade classroom where students have been exploring the relationship between addition and subtraction (a copy of the student assignment is available at More4U). During the last math session, two of the students, Luke and Jacob, made a conjecture that the class is working on proving today. Mrs. Sykes and the students are gathered in the whole-class meeting area (fig. 1.1)

Fig. 1.1. Create a central meeting place

as she poses the following task: "Luke and Jacob made a conjecture: You can use addition to solve subtraction, and you can use subtraction to solve addition problems. Do you agree or disagree with this conjecture? Prove your position using equations, words, and visual models."

STOP AND REFLECT

Before reading further, consider your stance. Do you agree or disagree with this conjecture? What tool or equation would you use to prove your response? Then, check to see how your response is similar to or different from the student responses that follow.

After Mrs. Sykes poses the task, students are given individual think time to consider their stance and to explain their thinking on paper. Students spread out, some working at tables, others at nooks and crannies around the room. Mrs. Sykes walks around documenting students' thinking in preparation for the later group discussion. After 10 minutes, Mrs. Sykes and the students gather around their meeting area to debrief (fig. 1.2). Mrs. Sykes asks students to give a thumbs up or down in agreement or disagreement with the conjecture. She calls on Esther, one of the quieter students in class, who had a claim similar to many of the students in the class in which she agreed with parts of the conjecture

Fig. 1.2. The class in discussion

and not with others. Esther says, "Addition can be used to solve subtraction, but subtraction can only be used to solve addition some of the time." As Esther shares, quite a few of the students nod their heads. John raises his hand and builds from Esther's comment, explaining that there are different addition problem types and that subtraction can be used only for certain ones.

Mrs. Sykes writes this claim on the whiteboard and instructs students to work in quads to investigate this, using physical and visual tools as well as equations. Groups spread out around the room with students frequently getting up to get resources—paper,

pencil, manipulatives—or walking to their math wall (a wall space documenting the big ideas and invented strategies discussed in class) to revisit strategies on addition and subtraction generated in the past month (see figs. 1.3 and 1.4).

The following day, the children meet with their teams to organize their findings and determine how they would present. Each team shares their work using the document camera. The majority of teams come to the same conclusion: "Yes, you can definitely add to subtract."

Fig. 1.3. Students solve problems on the math wall

Fig. 1.4. The math wall in use

Many prove this by using a number line modeling *Think Addition* (see below) to find the difference. They also conclude that you can subtract to add. In problem situations such as $43 + n = 67$, you could solve with $67 - 43 = n$. You could also use subtraction with $n + 24 = 67$ by solving $67 - 24 = n$. One team claims that you could also solve $43 + 24 = n$ with subtraction. The class has quite a discussion about that one because the majority of students feel that it did not make sense to them and wonder why you would do that when it is easier to just add the numbers. This conjecture is left on the "Burning Question" poster on the math wall for later discussion.

MAKING SENSE OF STUDENT THINKING: THINK ADDITION

Think Addition, a strategy students often use early on to solve subtraction problems, reflects the inverse relationship between addition and subtraction. For example, in the equation $13 - 3$, students would think, "What can I add to 3 to make 13?" to get a difference of 10. Learning about fact families is an important aspect of this strategy. When students realize that addition and subtraction equations can be formed with the same three numbers, they develop greater fluency with using these operations.

This vignette illustrates a problem-solving activity that builds from a conjecture that emerged from the previous lesson. Students were asked to develop their own stance, provide evidence for their response using models and equations, and receive and provide peer feedback. Throughout the lesson, students engaged in mathematics across group settings (individual, small group, whole class) and with different representations (context, words, physical tools, and symbols). The classroom layout and resources were organized to support how students and the teacher engaged in their investigation.

In the remainder of this chapter, we discuss some of the critical elements in designing an environment where the physical space can serve as a teaching tool. We provide illustrations of layouts and classroom photos as well as teacher commentaries and rationales for their design. The following elements of classroom design are discussed in detail: classroom layout, math walls, and learning resources.

The Physical Configuration

Fig. 1.5. Heidi Kwalk's fifth-grade classroom

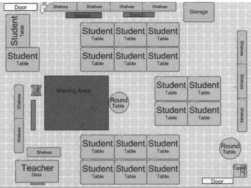

Fig. 1.6. Floor plan of Mrs. Kwalk's classroom

Fig. 1.7. Lauren Guite's first-grade classroom

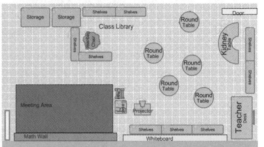

Fig. 1.8. Floor plan of Ms. Guite's classroom

STOP AND REFLECT

- Describe the physical arrangement of each of the two classrooms. How are the tables arranged? What types of space are available for varying types of group work (e.g., individual, partner, small group, whole class)? Where are learning resources and supplies stored?

- What is similar and what is different about the two rooms?

- What culture of learning is supported by each classroom layout?

The classrooms of Lauren Guite and Heidi Kwalk look different; however, both rooms are designed to support a common culture of learning that promotes students' individual and collective growth as mathematical thinkers. What are some features of these classrooms?

- Groups of desks to foster interaction
- Well-defined areas for working on the floor, at computers, alone, and as a group or whole class
- Easy access to learning resources and supplies—easy mobility from one workplace to another, to materials and supplies, to instructional resources on the walls

TEACHER COMMENTARY

I used to have individual desks but changed to tables. The students have their home spots where they come in the morning, but when they are working on reading or math workshop, they can work anywhere. It becomes a space for everyone. They are free to work at a table or get a clipboard and work on the rug. It's where they feel comfortable working. They collaborate and use and share the space more than when they first had their own designated spots.

—Lauren Guite, Grade 1

Although the room size and its shape, the number of students, and the available furniture influence the physical arrangements, attention to specific elements in the design of your physical space can help you promote interactions across learning resources. Organizing the classroom's physical space for active, interactive learning means creating well-defined spaces for individual, small-group, and whole-class discussions and providing easy access to learning resources. In addition, students must move easily from one work space to another and to mathematics tools and resources. Classroom transitions become smoother when students can efficiently navigate from one space to another during activities.

Designing space for mathematical community: Individual learning

Students need individual think time. The opportunity to think and wrestle with a problem independently encourages students' own sense making and perseverance as well as their self-esteem as mathematical thinkers. In most classrooms, students have an individual desk at which to work. Having easy access to clipboards allows students to move beyond their individual desks. An open space on the carpet, a pillow against the wall, or a small nook provides a quiet spot to work independently.

Designing space for mathematical community: Small-group learning

Figs. 1.9 and 1.10. Spaces for small groups

Collaborative learning requires that there be space for collaboration. Small, well-defined spaces encourage group interaction. Depending on the group size, such spaces can include rugs, tables, or benches (figs. 1.9 and 1.10).
When working in small groups, students need to be able to face each other to make communication easier. Having tools and materials (e.g., whiteboards, pencils, erasers, manipulatives, norms for student-to-student talk) nearby also promotes and supports productive interaction (fig. 1.11). Much time can be saved in the long run by taking time at the start of the school year to establish and practice routines for transitioning into and out of group work.

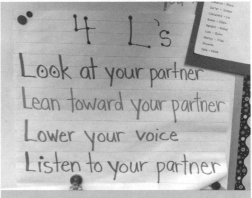

Fig. 1.11. Norms for communication

Designing space for mathematical community: Whole-class learning

The meeting area is a separate defined space for the class to gather. Students are more focused on the discussion if they are physically gathered close together. This is where the whole class has the opportunity to raise questions; share and defend their own models, ideas, and strategies; and create and argue solutions with one another. Students deepen their understanding of mathematics and their role as members of a learning community as they engage in collective activity, discourse, and reflection. The meeting area is often bordered by a wall and a whiteboard or chart board easel.

Figure 1.12 provides an example of a meeting area organized for whole-group discussion. Lauren Guite, a first-grade teacher in a Spanish Immersion classroom, uses an area rug to create a defined space for her whole-class discussions. The rug is

Fig. 1.12. Ms. Guite's meeting area

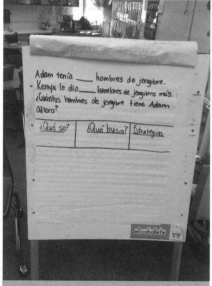

Fig. 1.13. An easel as focal point

placed next to a math wall where anchor charts and students' thinking are displayed. A chart paper easel is also placed next to the chair where she usually sits. The chart paper easel is where the students demonstrate their thinking and make comparisons between strategies and solution methods. The visual representation on the chart paper serves as a tool during their discussion. The chart paper is later moved to the math wall for future reference. Figure 1.13 provides an example of a chart Ms. Guite has created to introduce students to their problem of the day.

STRATEGIES FOR YOUR CLASSROOM

Lauren Guite is using a story structure for problem solving (see fig. 1.13) that is based on Cognitively Guided Instruction (CGI). Spaces for quantities are left blank intentionally to encourage students to look closely at the context and its meaning for problem solving. Here, Ms. Guite asks students to consider "What they already know," "What they're trying to figure out," and "Possible strategies for problem solving" before the quantities are even presented. Additional strategies for launching mathematics problems will be shared in Chapter 4.

The Math Wall

The math wall is a wall space devoted to mathematics. In the vignette of Mrs. Sykes's class, students used resources on the class math wall to reflect, compare, and build on previously learned concepts and student-generated strategies.

The math wall serves as a visual record of students' methods of problem solving (fig. 1.14) and should be used to engage students in discussing connections and relationships between prior ideas and new content. Students too often see mathematics activities as discrete lessons instead of seeing the coherence between them. Having direct access to prior learning promotes an explicit focus on the interconnection of mathematical ideas and how they build on one another.

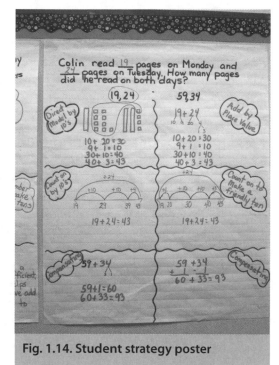

Fig. 1.14. Student strategy poster

Time constraints are another reason for saving student work. Time often seems to get the best of teachers when they are trying to orchestrate a rich discussion. Charting student work on poster paper makes it easy to continue the discussion the next day. Plus, a student may ask a rich question that should be pursued further, but there's limited time for investigation or the question is not directly related to the day's learning goal; putting the question on the math wall acknowledges its value and makes it easy to go back to it later (figs. 1.15 and 1.16).

Figs. 1.15 and 1.16. Burning question posters

Student thinking on display: What does it look like? How do I start?

Here we illustrate the use of the math wall as instructional space to reflect students' growing understanding and to share tools for problem solving and communication. The decision of what goes on the wall should be based on knowledge of the mathematical learning goals, students' needs, and their cognitive development.

> **MAKING SENSE OF STUDENT THINKING:**
> **EARLY DEVELOPMENT OF NUMBER CONCEPTS**
>
> Children's early development of number concepts moves from a concrete representation to the abstract. For example, students generally move from counting all (e.g., physically making four counters and then making twelve and counting all the counters to get sixteen), to counting on (e.g., starting at twelve and counting four to get to sixteen), to using part-whole (e.g., splitting apart the twelve to ten and two, adding the two to four, and then adding the ten to get sixteen), and finally to relational thinking (knowing that 6 + 10 is 16 so 6 + 9 would be just one less). Explicit discussions on student strategies and comparisons between strategies can support students in developing more efficient strategies.

In Ms. Guite's case, her understanding of children's progression from the concrete to the abstract guides decision making about what to include on the classroom math wall. The math wall is a reflection of the students' developing thinking and serves as a reference for students throughout their mathematical work. The charts and references created during class investigations and discussions and the student strategies on display represent varied approaches to problem solving. Ms. Guite intentionally selects strategies to include concrete representations (e.g., the use of base-ten blocks to solve 24 + 19) as well as abstract representations (e.g., compensation strategy where 59 + 34 becomes 60 + 33). This is purposeful, and these displays are constantly referenced during whole-group interactions, as when students are encouraged to consider the relationship between strategies and the efficiency of the strategy used in relation to the problem posed.

Mrs. Sykes's math wall is bare at the start of the school year. From the first day, she lets students know that posters of their thinking will be added to reflect their growing knowledge, understandings, and conjectures (see fig. 1.17). The wall is kept at eye level so students can make reference to it during their own think time. Student strategies are first displayed with the student's name (e.g., "Saul's strategy") and later labeled with formal academic terms so the mathematical language is linked to meaning.

Fig. 1.17. Mrs. Sykes's math wall

TEACHING TIP: STUDENTS' STRATEGIES

When strategies are first shared, write the students' name next to the strategy (e.g., "Saul's strategy"). This provides easy reference back to the strategy and encourages student dialogue. For example, if a student wants to try out Saul's strategy, she or he can talk directly to Saul. Once students are familiar with the strategy, introduce the formal academic term for it. Developing academic language within context builds a stronger cognitive bond, making it more likely students will know and use it appropriately and with greater precision (Moschkovich 1999; Planas and Civil 2013).

An instructional wall: Supporting norms for doing mathematics

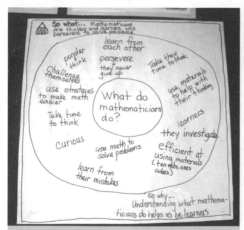

Fig. 1.18. Norms for engaging with mathematics as mathematicians

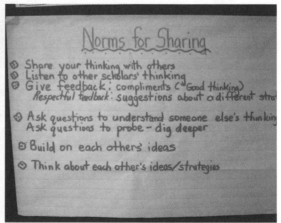

Fig. 1.19. Norms for student talk

Before students can actively engage with the mathematics and with each other, norms for engagement need to be established. Teachers cultivate classroom norms in many different ways. It's important to pay attention to the norms you want to foster in your classroom and to make these norms explicit to your students. Set up norms for students to engage with the mathematics and their peers. Then, post a classroom poster of these norms near the whole-class meeting area to support students as they learn how to talk and engage in the mathematics and with each other's ideas (see figs. 1.18 and 1.19). (See Chapter 2 for more about strategies to develop classroom norms and to promote student math talks.)

A math focus wall

The math focus wall is an interactive mathematics bulletin board that reflects the daily learning in the classroom. It is often used in a ten- to fifteen-minute warm-up, and its purpose is to provide students with an opportunity to deepen their understanding of core concepts of mathematics at their grade level. In the mini-lesson, several tools, representations, and models are used to support students' thinking about connections between representations to operations.

Vanessa Frank, who teaches a kindergarten/first-grade combination class, reserves wall space near her whole-class meeting area for her math focus wall. Each day, Ms. Frank selects two or three problems that target specific content and process standards at her grade level. Problem solving and academic language use are integral in the activity.

Video clip 1.1, Math Wall Lesson, (available at More4U) shows Ms. Frank using the math focus wall to engage students in discussion around subtraction, place-value models, and decomposing a ten. Examine the nature of the conversation. How does the wall space serve as an instructional tool for Ms. Frank and her students? Why did Ms. Frank provide a story for the subtraction problem? What teaching strategies are used to reveal student thinking and encourage thoughtful responses?

Video: Math Wall Lesson (See More4U.)

Instructional walls: What else?

Heidi Kwalk develops fraction and decimal meaning from students' understanding of whole-number place value. To create a large place-value chart, she uses a row of cabinet doors with each door representing one of the positions in the place-value system (fig. 1.20).

She uses this to support students' understanding of the 10-to-1 relationship between the value of any two adjacent positions. This 10-to-1 relationship can extend infinitely in both directions. One hundred is the same as 10 tens, just as one-tenth is the same as 10 hundredths.

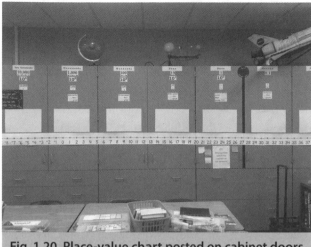

Fig. 1.20. Place-value chart posted on cabinet doors

Darielle Tom, who teaches a kindergarten/first-grade combination class, gives each student her or his own space on the classroom math wall (see figs. 1.21 and 1.22). Dr. Tom conferences with each student to decide what should be added to this wall space. The wall space serves as a resource for students to reflect on strategies learned, and it provides a visual documentation of their mathematical growth throughout the year.

Fig. 1.21. Student work on math wall

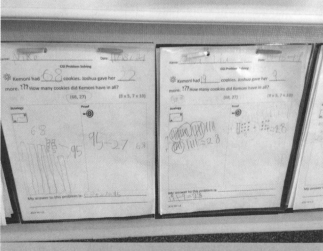

Fig. 1.22. Student work on math wall

Tools and Supplies

In the vignettes presented throughout this chapter, the students used mathematical tools and supplies during their independent think time and when proving their conjectures in their small groups. Students needed easy access to these materials to ensure that the flow of the mathematical inquiry is not interrupted while students or the teacher retrieves materials. Also, when tools are not easily accessible, students are less likely to use them.

> **TEACHING TIP: SELECTING THE RIGHT TOOL**
>
> Once a problem is assigned, instruct students to think about how they will approach the problem and the tool that would best support and represent this approach. Asking students to take the time to reflect about matching tools and resources to a specific strategy prevents the whole class from rushing to the supplies at the same time and encourages students to be more strategic in their selection.

Teaching and learning resources consist of two types: those used by us, the teachers, and those used by the students. Teacher resources should be stored inside a closet or on high shelves. Student resources should be kept low and be easily visible and accessible.

The shelves in figure 1.23 contain different resources that are easily accessible to the teacher and students. Labeled or clear containers enable students to quickly see what kinds of tools are available and know where to return them after use. Having clearly defined spaces for mathematical tools and resources (e.g., counting collections, counters, materials for math centers, writing materials, measuring tools) will ease access and prevent crowding.

Fig. 1.23. Storage for math tools

Thoughts about tool selection and use

> An excellent mathematics program integrates the use of mathematical tools and technology as essential resources to help students learn and make sense of mathematical ideas, reason mathematically, and communicate their mathematical thinking. (NCTM 2014a, p. 78)

As you think about the range of tools to make available to students, consider how these tools (including technologies) may both support students' growth toward specific mathematical learning goals and increase access to demonstrate their mathematical thinking (King-Sears 2009; Pritchard, O'Hara, and Zwiers 2014; Sarama and Clements 2009; Suh and Moyer 2007). Although it is often best to allow students to choose the tools they want to use in a mathematical activity (Moyer and Jones 2004), there are times when teachers will find it useful to prescribe the tool choices. For example, when fifth-grade teacher Mayra Orozco found that many of her students had a fragile understanding of decimal numbers and were unable to translate between various representations, she designed a lesson that required students to rotate individually through the use of several tools, including base-ten blocks, coins, and 100-grids. The culminating activity challenged students to find connections among the various representations that helped them to better understand decimal numbers. See Chapter 4 on assessment for more about this lesson.

Figs. 1.24–1.27. Make materials accessible.

Digital learning spaces

Most schools now provide digital learning spaces to complement the physical space of the classroom (and some schools are entirely digital). Teachers must think about how to make use of digital tools and resources to support students' learning of mathematics in ways aligned with curricular goals (Pritchard, O'Hara, and Zwiers 2014; Sarama and Clements 2009). For instance, class websites offer a place to post resources for reference, review, and exploration. When posting resources to a class website, teachers should consider how well aligned these are to the way in which they want students to come to understand mathematical ideas and skills. Just as keeping desks in rows can work against the development of rich mathematical collaboration and discourse, posting videos showing how to perform an algorithm without any sense making or linking to games requiring minimal mathematical reasoning can disrupt efforts to create a community of mathematics learners engaged in practices of reasoning, sense making, explanation, and justification.

TECHNOLOGY INTEGRATION

Desiree Olivas uses Google Classroom to provide varied opportunities for students to share their thinking and respond to others' ideas. At times students are encouraged and prompted to respond to and expand on each other's thinking on an online forum. Other times, students use Sketchpad or watch or create their own videos explaining a mathematics concept or problem.

In addition, an ever-growing proportion of students have ready access to handheld computing devices, such as smartphones and tablets, and routinely use these for social purposes (Project Tomorrow 2011). These digital tools can be used to promote productive collaboration and communication through activities such as blog posts about recent mathematical tasks, screencasts of student problem solving, and shared images of mathematics in students' communities; such activities have the potential to increase engagement among a wide range of students (King-Sears 2009; Pritchard, O'Hara, and Zwiers 2014; Roschelle et al. 2010). And remember, just as norms help govern students' productive interactions in the physical classroom, it is important to establish and enforce norms for interactions in digital spaces (Ribble 2012). Throughout the remaining chapters, we include examples of the productive use of tools and technology within the context of establishing powerful mathematics learning environments.

Summary and Reflection

The vignettes in this chapter demonstrate ways that the strategic organization and use of a classroom's physical and virtual space can support rich mathematics learning. The classroom setting lays the foundation for all the other elements of the learning environment: discourse, task, assessments, and families and communities. A rich physical and virtual environment should have well-defined spaces for individual, small-group, and whole-class work and easy access to learning resources (i.e., other students and the teacher, tools and supplies, and spaces displaying student and class work).

STRATEGIES FOR YOUR CLASSROOM

Considerations for Designing Your Physical Environment

The physical configuration

- Well-defined spaces for individual, small-group, and whole-class learning where students can easily see each other
- Clear paths for mobility from one place to another (e.g., meeting area to individual seats)
- Easy access to learning resources (e.g., whiteboards, pencils, manipulatives, and norms for mathematics engagement)

The math wall

- Wall space to display student strategies, conjectures, and norms for engagement
- Clear path and easy access to the math wall
- Wall at eye level for students (not the teacher)

Tools/supplies

- Clearly defined spaces for mathematical tools, including manipulatives
- Easy access to student resources
- Labels or clear containers to facilitate return of materials and allow for easier accounting
- Separate spaces for resources to prevent overcrowding

Before you move on to the next chapter, take a moment to reflect on these questions:

STOP AND REFLECT

Consider pairing with another teacher to observe the structural setup in each other's classrooms:

- What type of space is available for students to work independently, in pairs, in small groups, and as a whole class?

- Do these spaces have easy access to—

    o manipulatives, tools, and general supplies?

    o norms to engage in the mathematics and with each other (e.g., norms for engagement, sentence starters for student talk)?

    o a variety of work spaces including digital ones?

- What wall spaces (and digital spaces) are available to share student thinking?

Make time to discuss the observations. Plan any changes accordingly.

Chapter 2

The Discourse-Rich Environment

> Effective teaching of mathematics facilitates discourse among students to build shared understanding of mathematical ideas by analyzing and comparing student approaches and arguments.
>
> —National Council of Teachers of Mathematics (NCTM),
> *Principles to Actions: Ensuring Mathematical Success for All*

Communication with and about mathematics plays a central role in a rich learning environment. Students learn more and more deeply by explaining their own thinking and engaging with others' thinking. Meaningful engagement with mathematics "includes the purposeful exchange of ideas through classroom discussion, as well as through other forms of verbal, visual, and written communication" (NCTM 2014a). Such practices encourage students to monitor their own thinking, see similarities and differences, make connections, extend understandings, and generate new ideas.

WHAT'S VALUED?

Richard, a fourth-grade student, came home with a long worksheet of subtraction problems to solve using a common standard algorithm. His mother noticed that he got an incorrect answer on every problem. Richard was content with finishing his homework, yet his mother was concerned not only about errors but about his apparent lack of sense making in doing this work.

She said to Richard, "Let's talk about this. Is there another way you could work out these problems?" Richard thought about it for a minute and then identified two other strategies that made sense to him—using base-ten blocks to model the problem and counting up by numbers. His mother encouraged him to use these strategies to illustrate his thinking. Richard responded that none of that would matter in class; homework was passed to a neighbor, and answers were marked right or wrong. Richard added that the other methods took too long; his teacher often said that students should get the answers quickly.

Reflect: How do the discourse patterns in Richard's math class impact his thinking about what it means to learn math and whose ideas matter in math class?

As long as the answer is correct – your thinking process is not valued.

We cannot make productive mathematical discourse happen merely by placing students in desks that face each other, telling students to write out their thinking, or asking a few volunteers to share their ideas. It is quite possible that students who have not had meaningful opportunities to engage in mathematical discourse may not know how to participate: what to say or show, what is expected, and how to explain their thinking. Students need a supportive environment that cultivates trust and positions them as capable, confident contributors to the emerging mathematical understanding in the classroom.

In the previous chapter, we discussed the relationship between the physical attributes of the classroom and the type of interactions that are possible; this chapter focuses on these interactions and the importance of establishing norms and routines for students to engage in meaningful communication across participation structures. We present considerations for designing a discourse-rich learning environment through three participation structures: individual engagement, small-group interactions, and whole-class discussions.

Before reading further, take a moment to think about the opportunities for student discourse in the following example.

A Peek Inside a Classroom

Jennifer Lawyer's fourth-grade class gathers on the rug. She starts her daily math time with a math talk to support students in mathematical discourse and strengthen their number sense and reasoning. Ms. Lawyer writes $8 \times \frac{1}{3} = m + \frac{2}{3}$ on the board.

Ms. Lawyer: What would make this equation true? Eight times one-third is the same as m plus two-thirds. I want you to take a few minutes to think on your own. When you are ready to share, put your thumb up on your knee.

[Ms. Lawyer gives students two minutes of think time and scans the room acknowledging the varied ways in which students approach the problem.]

Ms. Lawyer: Good job. I see Esther skip-counting on her fingers. Nice strategy. Isabel, I see you scrunching your eyebrows. I know you can make sense of this, so take some time to look at it and think about it a little bit more.

[To the class:]

Raise your hand if you need a few more minutes.

[About a third of the students raise their hands.]

Ms. Lawyer: Take your time. I will give you more time to think.

[Ms. Lawyer gives one more minute of wait time.]

Ms. Lawyer: What could be the value of m? OK. Before you turn and talk, I want to give you something else to think about. Do you predict that m will be greater or less than three-thirds?

[Ms. Lawyer waits approximately 30 seconds.]

Ms. Lawyer: Will m be greater or less than three-thirds? Turn and talk with your partner and see what ideas you can come up with. Go ahead and turn and talk—and remember to be an active listener as well.

[*During partner talk, students discuss solutions, and Ms. Lawyer circulates among them, listening to their thinking, making notes about students she might call on later, and stepping into the conversations to pose questions meant to push students' reasoning.*]

Tracy: Three one-thirds is one whole. And if you put three more one-thirds, that's another whole. So that makes two wholes. So it's two wholes and two more thirds.

Ms. Lawyer: So let's see. Esther, you said m is six-thirds, and Tracy, are you saying m is two wholes? So I wonder who is right? Six-thirds or two wholes? Are those the same?

Esther: Yes.

Ms. Lawyer: How do you know, Esther? Can you show me?

Esther: Because three-thirds equals a whole and if it was six-thirds, that would equal two wholes.

Ms. Lawyer: So what does that mean? Do you guys have the same answer?

Tracy: Yeah, but in a different form.

Ms. Lawyer: Nice work, girls.

[*During the whole-class discussion:*]

Ms. Lawyer: Raise your hand if you revised your thinking a little more after talking to your partner.

[*The majority of the students in class raise their hands.*]

Ms. Lawyer: Nice. All right, who would like to share today?

[*After one student shares his thinking for two wholes and another student shares his thinking for why m equaled six-thirds:*]

Ms. Lawyer: Does anyone have any questions so far?

Isabel: Joseph said m is two and Julio is thinking m is six-thirds. I wonder if these are the same.

Tracy: I was thinking about the same question.

[handwritten margin note: facilitation of discussion that enable students to compare and contrast quantities / solutions]

Ms. Lawyer: So I guess we have a few different answers for *m*. Why don't you take another minute with your partner to talk about this. See if you can convince each other.

[*The class erupts into excited discussion about this. Many students are drawing diagrams on their whiteboards, some are showing bar models, and others are working with numerical representations.*]

Ms. Lawyer: So what did you come up with? Can both of these values for *m* be correct? Isabel, you first posed the question, so let's start with you.

The discussion continues with students sharing their use of different models and equations to prove the equivalence of six-thirds (Julio's answer) and two wholes (Joseph's). A complete transcript of the discussion can be found at More4U.

Ms. Lawyer uses classroom talk to deepen students' understanding of fraction equivalence. This activity builds on students' prior work and understanding of unit fractions and fractional wholes. Students are given multiple opportunities to formulate, explain, and refine their thinking as they engage in independent, pair, and whole-group discourse. Ms. Lawyer is strategic in her use of wait time and questioning to probe, scaffold, and extend students' thinking. For example, she calls on particular students to share and intentionally brings up the question of comparing Joseph's and Julio's thinking to highlight its equivalence.

In the remainder of this chapter, we share specific strategies and considerations to support student discourse and to promote equitable participation.

Considerations for Students' Engagement in Discourse

Before we address norms and routines related to specific participation structures, we need to examine some general considerations about supporting every student in mathematical discourse.

Power and participation

Classrooms must be safe places where students feel they belong and are seen as capable contributors whose ideas are valued (Engle and Conant 2002; NCTM 2014a). This inclusivity makes it possible for students to take risks, discuss and debate ideas, and share partial and even incorrect understandings publicly. When thinking about cultivating such an environment, teachers must notice and address issues of power and status.

Teachers play a major role in establishing and distributing (and disrupting) power relations in the classroom. This may be made explicit by the class norms and routines that are set and enforced. However, this also occurs in more subtle ways: the responses selected to be publicly shared (correct answers and strategies or incorrect solutions and partial understandings), the problem-solving processes and strategies encouraged and valued (only eliciting limited perspectives or encouraging a broad range of approaches), and the sorts of problems assigned for students to solve (prescribing all of the work or allowing flexibility and choice). Which students the teachers select to publicly share and how teachers respond to student errors and ideas send important messages about the culture of learning fostered and how student contributions are valued.

Power and status are also communicated in the way teachers denote students' potential. For instance, referring to students as "low" or "struggling" implies a difference in status and potential for learning that often results in limiting the full participation of these students (Horn 2007). Each of us authors (and the teachers from whom we draw the examples in this book) has had in our classrooms students who came in with deficit-focused labels based on state test data and other reports and who, when nurtured to participate in discourse-rich, meaning-centered learning communities, flourished as mathematical thinkers.

Language use and development

Language plays a critical role in discourse (Razfar, Khisty, and Chval 2011). It is important for teachers to think about how to best leverage students' strengths while recognizing their areas for growth. For example, English language learners (ELLs), who are simultaneously learning mathematics content and English linguistics, should be allowed to use their native languages as well as English during their investigation of mathematical concepts and relationships (Moschkovich 1999; Planas and Civil 2013).

TEACHING TIP: VOCABULARY DEVELOPMENT

Vocabulary is more deeply understood and retained in a student's long-term memory when it is learned *after* he or she has engaged in some exploration of the idea or relationship it represents. Cognitively connecting a known concept to specific academic language ensures understanding and increases students' ability to use language with precision.

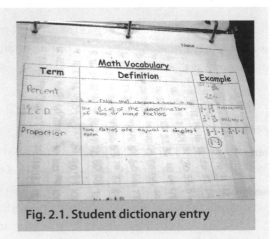

Fig. 2.1. Student dictionary entry

For all students, academic language is challenging to learn because it may not be part of students' everyday experience outside of school. The teaching of academic language in mathematics must be intentional, embedded in context and meaning, and done with attention to precision (see Teaching Tip: Vocabulary Development). This includes awareness of mathematical terms as students are developing conceptual and procedural knowledge as well as opportunities for students to practice using academic language to reinforce understanding. Here are some strategies for scaffolding each student's participation in mathematical discourse:

- Use student-made dictionaries to link concepts and terms with drawings and examples (see the example in fig. 2.1 and More4U for a student dictionary template).

- Allow students to code-switch (move between their native language and English) when expressing their ideas.

- Use and allow students to use visuals and real objects to bring meaning to concepts, relationships, and problem-solving scenarios.

- Display word walls, including visuals and translations, to assist students in verbal conversations and writing.

- Provide daily opportunities for students to use academic language in context to explain and justify their thinking in writing and speech.

- Use math journals in which students record solution strategies and thought processes and write about their learning.

Math journals can be used to record a student's solutions and his or her thought processes to arrive at a solution or as a reflection of student learning. Because the entries are dated, the journal documents the student's growth in strategy development and mathematical thinking over time. Figures 2.2–4 document Evelyn's math work in September, October, and December. Throughout the fall, she progressed from direct modeling, drawing every object in the problem, to using more relational strategies (using tens and twenties). Her journal documented her growth.

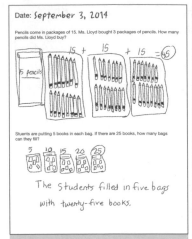

Fig. 2.2. Evelyn's journal entries, from Alicia Lloyd's third-grade class (a)

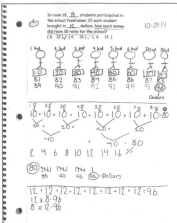

Fig. 2.3. Evelyn's journal entries, from Alicia Lloyd's third-grade class (b)

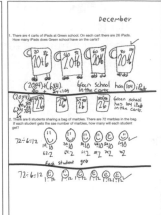

Fig. 2.4. Evelyn's journal entries, from Alicia Lloyd's third-grade class (c)

Routines and Habits to Support Mathematical Discourse

Routines can help support students in actively engaging in their own and others' learning. Consider our example of Ms. Lawyer's fourth-grade classroom: she followed a routine co-created with two of her colleagues, Alicia Lloyd and Vanessa Hayward:

1. Provide a mathematical prompt/task.

2. Read the prompt to students.

3. Give quiet, independent time to make sense of the problem.

4. Recommend perseverance in working through confusion.

5. Commend students for taking time to think, make connections, and revise their ideas.

6. Have students turn and talk with a partner.

7. Ask, "Who agreed with their partner?" Then, "Who changed their thinking as a result of their conversation?"

8. Provide whole-class share with occasional partner talk if needed.

Although this is not the only routine that could work, this set of actions provide a daily structure for Ms. Lawyer and her students to generate, share, and deepen their understandings of mathematics.

Routines alone do not ensure that the discussion will be focused on students' mathematical thinking. In some classrooms, despite routines that promote discourse, it is the teacher's thinking or that of only a handful of students that dominates. In order to avoid this pitfall, teachers and students need to learn to use discourse habits that distribute opportunities to contribute and make students' ideas the focus of discussion.

Fortunately, there are specific habits that have been shown to be particularly effective in promoting rich discourse. Suzanne Chapin, Catherine O'Connor, and Nancy Anderson (2009) in *Classroom Discussions* describe five "talk moves" (see table 2.1 and More4U for a downloadable copy) that can serve as a guide for both teacher and student talk. Think about placing a poster of talk moves (fig. 2.5) near the meeting area where the whole-class discussion takes place. The poster can serve as a visual tool to support students in initiating discourse during small-group or whole-class settings.

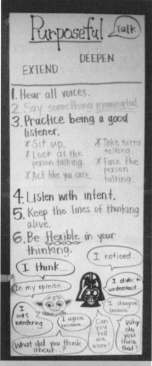

Fig. 2.5. Purposeful talk poster

Table 2.1. Talk moves to support discourse

Move/habit	Explanation and use
Revoicing "So, you're saying . . ."	• Repeat some or all of what the student said; then ask the student to respond and verify whether the revoicing is correct. • Revoicing can be used to clarify or highlight an idea.
Repeating "Can you repeat what he said in your own words?" "Can someone say that in a different way?"	• Ask a student to repeat or rephrase another student's idea. • Repeating encourages students to listen closely to others and allows more time to consider important ideas.

Continued on page 28

Table 2.1. (continued)

Reasoning "Do you agree or disagree—and why?"	• After students have time to process another student's idea, ask students to analyze someone else's claim. • Refrain from supporting one position or another. • Ask students to explain "why" to encourage them to apply their thinking to someone else's contribution. • Reasoning allows students to engage in each other's ideas.
Building on "Does someone want to say something more about that?" "Does someone want to raise any questions about the point made?"	• Prompt students to expand on the idea already stated. • "Building on" validates student contributions and allows more perspectives to be considered.
Wait time "Take your time . . . we'll wait."	• Wait at least 10 seconds after asking a question before calling on someone for an answer. • Wait at least the same amount of time after calling on a student to give the student time to process and organize his or her thoughts.

allowing enough time to think — NO RUSH HERE

Source: Adapted from Chapin, O'Connor, and Anderson (2009)

Participation Structures to Support Mathematics Discourse

Students need to engage in discussion across different types of participation structures: individual think time, partner or small-group talk, and whole-group discussion.

Individual think time

Individual think time is particularly helpful before partner, small-group, or whole-class sharing. For many students, particularly for English-language learners or students reluctant to share with others, this one- to two-minute time period is invaluable. Allowing each student time to think—and to write down her or his thinking—before sharing promotes greater participation. Encourage students to use representations such as diagrams, symbolic expressions, and words to explain and justify their thinking. These representations serve as tools during discussion because they provide a shared visual to help understand a student's explanation.

I like this idea

Fig. 2.6. Independent think time

Figure 2.7 Student pair share

Figures 2.6 and 2.7 offer an example of one way to afford individual think time followed by pair share. Christine Bouma, a fifth-grade teacher, has student pairs sit back to back. Students are first given a few minutes of individual think time to write down their thinking. Then, students turn to face their partner and share.

TECHNOLOGY INTEGRATION

Discourse extends beyond verbal talk. Elementary students can also construct arguments using concrete referents such as drawings and diagrams. Desmos, Geometer's Sketchpad, and GeoGebra are three examples of mathematics visualization software that can be used to support students in making sense of concepts or procedures and in exploring mathematical ideas as they observe, make, and test conjectures about mathematical relationships.

Small-group discourse

Students who learn to articulate and justify their own mathematical ideas, reason through their own and others' mathematical explanations, and provide a rationale for their own answers develop a deep understanding that is critical to their future success in mathematics and related fields (Carpenter, Franke, and Levi 2003, p.6).

Collaboration on tasks that promote reasoning and problem solving can enhance students' mathematical thinking (Michaels, O'Connor, and Resnick 2008). Through working with others, students can deepen their own understanding as they examine mathematical ideas and problems from various perspectives. Small-group settings can foster peer interdependence, as students learn to interact with each other and rely less on the teacher.

Productive group interactions

Simply placing students in collaborative groups does not ensure that all students will engage in mathematically meaningful conversations. It is common to see a range of interactions during group work: from students learning together as a group, to students working individually, to one student "expert" dominating the interaction (Cohen et al. 1999; Esmonde 2009; Weissglass 2002). Creating a culture of shared responsibility and equal participation requires strategic planning.

Grouping strategies

Determining how students are grouped requires careful attention. Working strategically with students at a particular level of readiness can be helpful. However, continual grouping solely by prior achievement (which is often mistakenly equated with ability) results in uneven levels of participation and has been shown to widen the achievement gap (National Education Association 2015). Instead, consider using flexible grouping, in which the size and makeup are determined by the following questions: "What is the learning outcome of this activity, and what composition of students within each group will best support them in meeting this learning outcome?" This instructional strategy draws on teachers' knowledge of the mathematics goals and of their students' individual characteristics. Some examples of what this might look like—aligning student grouping strategies with learning goals—are given, along with suggested ways to structure the discourse:

Grouping by student-generated solutions and strategies

- Find two people who used a strategy similar to yours to solve the problem. How are your strategies similar? How are they different? What made you think to use this strategy? How did it help you solve the problem?

- Find someone who used a different strategy to solve the problem. Share your strategies. When you share your strategy, your job is to help your partner see what you did mathematically. If you are the listener, your job is to try to understand your partner's strategy. What are the mathematical connections between your strategy and that of your partner?

Grouping based on number choice or problem type

- Find a partner who either worked on the same type of problem but with different number choices or worked on a different type of problem but with similar number choices. Can you pose a question to your partner to get him or her to elaborate on the strategy used? What new ideas do you have after talking with your partner? What might you try next time you see a problem like this or work with numbers like this?

Grouping to consider alternative solutions and revise

- Find someone who got a different answer than you. Can you explain your partner's reasoning? What did you learn from talking with your partner?

Norms for small-group discourse

The participation dynamics we often see during whole-group discussion (which we discuss later) also play out in small-group settings. Left unchecked, students who are quick to raise their hands and share publicly tend to dominate small-group interactions. It is important for teachers to work with students to establish norms and expectations that reflect a sense of shared responsibility; every student's learning is important, and therefore all students must be given opportunities to meaningfully contribute to the mathematical discourse within the group.

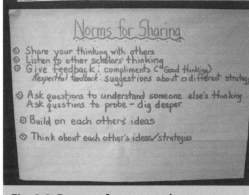

Fig. 2.8. Poster of co-created norms

Take time at the start of the school year to have a discussion about norms; this tells students that every student's participation is important in forming a discourse community.

Routines for small-group discourse

The quality of the group collaboration often mirrors the classroom discourse (Esmonde 2009; N. M. Webb et al., 2014). Therefore, promoting equitable participation in collaborative group structures requires a shift in the teacher's role. When a group member seeks help or asks a question, pose the question back to the whole group. This communicates to students the importance of taking ownership of their learning and of negotiating meanings rather than relying on the teacher's authority. Also, when you check in on group progress, rather than asking students to explain their strategy, ask them to explain or justify the strategy of another member of the group.

keep track of participation

TEACHING TIP: ACCOUNTABILITY IN GROUP WORK

In group work where students are collaboratively problem solving on paper, give each member a different color marker. This color-coding offers a visual for students to gauge and monitor their participation and contribution. View a photo of a student example at More4U.

Routines need to be established to ensure that all members of the group are participating and that all student contributions are included. Some suggestions are provided below.

Group roles

A key to successful group work is individual accountability. Group roles can establish individual accountability and a shared responsibility for the learning. The purpose of the roles is to give each student a clear way to participate in the group activity and conversation. Go to More4U for more resources on group roles. Prior to the start of group work, review the norms and expectations for participation. Student participation is scaffolded through having an explicit expectation for the group's success.

Conversational Prompting

For many students, prior experiences with math discussions centered on reporting out an answer to a calculation or explanations of procedural steps. If we want mathematical conversations to evolve to include sharing ideas, reasoning, and sense making, students need models for how to contribute meaningfully to different types of discussions. Students learn what to share when prompted to articulate important parts of their explanations. Talk starters or conversational prompts can help students consider what and how to share. The conversational prompts also serve as language support, particularly helpful for English learners and more reticent students, to enter into small- and whole-group conversation. Have related vocabulary and sentence frames at a place easily accessible, such as students' math folders (see fig. 2.9 and More4U) or a poster placed in easy view of all students.

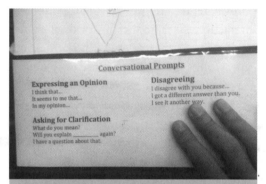

Fig. 2.9. Conversational prompts

Focused Student Pairings

Focused student pairings provide a set amount of time for each student to share his or her thinking without interruption. Time is explicitly devoted to making sure that each person has an equal chance to talk before the other can respond.

mediator (timer)

LOVE THIS!

TECHNOLOGY INTEGRATION

Screencasting apps, such as ScreenChomp, Educreations, and Doceri, give students space to draw pictures, annotate an image, and narrate their problem-solving steps. David Rhodes uses screencasting to have his sixth-grade students examine and reason about each other's problem solving. First, groups are tasked with creating a demonstration video of their problem solving using visual representations and mathematical notation but without audio (see screenshot in fig. 2.10). Then, groups are given the video created by another group and tasked with developing and recording a voice-over explanation of the work shown. This activity requires students to reason through others' mathematical ideas and articulate their reasoning.

Fig. 2.10. One group's recorded demonstration

Whole-Class Discussions

Whole-class discussions are critical in developing an environment where students can share and learn from each other's strategies and ideas. The mathematical goal serves as the compass that guides the classroom talk. Mathematical discussions can center around concepts, procedures, representations, reasoning, and explanations. The aim is for students to reflect on their own learning while attending to the logic within the ideas of others. Hence, the focus is on understanding students' ideas, not on correcting their answers. This does not mean that teachers should deemphasize correct answers. However, it is important for students to have opportunities to practice their reasoning in discussions without immediate attention to whether the answer is correct. By doing so, students become more confident in their ability to focus on sense making of concepts, skills, and problems, and they gradually lose some of the anxiety associated with the focus on being "right" or "wrong."

TECHNOLOGY INTEGRATION

Ruth Freedman-Finch teaches a second/third-grade combination class. She sometimes begins a task launch by providing the answer to a multiple-step problem with the goal of encouraging students to go beyond the answer (since it's already provided) and to attend to their process of problem solving and reasoning. A quick response code (commonly referred to as a QR code) is given that links to the answer. Students can use their iPads to scan and check their answers any time during the task exploration (see fig. 2.11 and More4U to view Mrs. Freedman-Finch's task launch).

Fig. 2.11. A student scans the QR code and checks her answer

One of the most critical challenges in leading whole-class discussions is to actually bring the whole class into the discussion. Teachers need to facilitate and guide mathematical conversation without being the sole deliverer of information or the primary evaluator of mathematical correctness. In a community of learners, meaning must be developed, explored, and negotiated together as mathematical thinking is shared publicly. Establishing norms and routines helps students know how to participate in a discursive community. In addition, teachers must carefully and purposefully facilitate discourse that builds on student thinking and guide the learning of the class toward the lesson's mathematical goals.

Developing norms for whole-class discourse

First and foremost, the teacher must establish clear ground rules to create the conditions for respectful talk and equitable participation. If students are afraid that their ideas will be ridiculed, they will not talk freely. They must feel that their classroom is a safe place to express their thoughts and questions and to take risks. Even one hostile or disrespectful interchange must be immediately addressed so it does not hamper students' willingness to openly share.

Just as with small-group discourse, teacher and students should co-construct whole-class discussion norms by defining what productive, inclusive interactions look like, sound like, and feel like. Establishing classroom norms begins on the first day of class, but they may be refined as needed to reflect a culture of shared responsibility for learning.

A Peek Inside a Classroom

Let's revisit Marie Sykes classroom from Chapter 1 to illustrate one teacher's approach to supporting the co-construction of such a culture. At the start of the 2015–2016 school year, Mrs. Sykes spent the first week of school co-creating the classroom norms with her students. On the first day, she asked the class to generate a list of norms to support their individual learning as well as the growth of the classroom community. Each day following, Mrs. Sykes started the mathematics session by reviewing the rules/expectations for engagement established by the class to ensure that the norms were clear and explicit. At the end of each math session, Mrs. Sykes led students to reflect on their created norms, and the norms were modified on the basis of classroom reflection. After four days of discussion, she noted that the norms generated had not addressed students' roles for engaging with each other. If students have not had opportunities to experience deep levels of peer engagement, they may need to see it in action. Therefore, Mrs. Sykes showed a video of two of her students from the previous year engaging in mathematical communication in order to spark a conversation with her current students about what they noticed and viewed as important in the partner talk.

The video clip Discussing Group Discussion Norms (available at More4U), shows Mrs. Sykes and the students, after they had viewed the video, in a conversation about what it means to meaningfully engage in group discussion. Examine the nature of the conversation. What are some norms Mrs. Sykes communicates to her students as she asks for students to share their thinking? What do you think students are learning about how to engage in mathematical conversation?

Video: Discussing group discussion norms (See More4U.)

For a teacher, it takes skill and practice to initiate a whole-class discussion about students' mathematical thinking and facilitate it in such a way that students are guided toward specific mathematical learning goals. Deciding what idea to start with requires much thought. And once you have sparked discussion, it takes skill to manage both the mathematical ideas under consideration and students' participation in this. We offer strategies to address these two challenges.

Selecting strategies to share

Whole-class discussions should be driven by students' mathematical thinking. The selection of what to share—whose ideas and for what purpose or purposes—is important and must be intentional (Kazemi and Hintz 2014; M. Smith and Stein 2011). There are varied ways to have students share their strategies. In order to make multiple strategies and approaches explicit for others to learn from, teachers can select students to share strategies for solving problems. For example, you may choose student presentations to highlight new strategies or to compare and contrast two or more different strategies. You may want to position a specific student as a competent contributor to whole-class dialogue, especially if that student has not had an opportunity to share. You may select a partial strategy to get a good start to a problem and then have the class finish it together. In Chapter 3, you will have an opportunity to see two classrooms engaged in the same math task; each classroom discussion was led differently on the basis of the learning goals each teacher had for students.

Developing Classroom Routines

Some students are ready to share their mathematical ideas, while others may be more hesitant. It is important to foster a safe environment for risk taking. Routines, such as the following, are essential to ensure that students are actively involved and accountable to each other in mathematical dialogue during whole-group shares:

- **Ideas belong to the group:** Once an idea is offered by a student, it is open for conversation among her or his classmates.

- **Anticipation/conjectures:** When a student is sharing, stop during the explanation, and ask questions to spark conjectures from classmates about what they think might happen next or why that student decided to start the strategy in that way.

- **Error analysis:** As students share their strategies, other students might notice places where they made mistakes in their own work. Teachers can develop routines of asking about, celebrating, and growing from mistakes. Reflections on errors are an opportunity for learning.

Strategy sharing in whole-group settings can help students learn and make connections among mathematical concepts. But once students' ideas are offered up for discussion, the teacher's role becomes that of sustaining productive discourse. There are a variety of questioning strategies that can help.

Asking Purposeful Questions

In effective teaching, teachers use a variety of question types to assess and gather evidence of student thinking, including questions that gather information, probe understanding, make the mathematics visible, and ask students to reflect on and justify their reasoning. (NCTM 2014a, p. 41).

As discussed earlier, teachers and students should use talk moves to nurture an environment where students feel comfortable sharing their ideas, are okay with mistakes, and listen closely to the ideas of their peers. Along with talk moves, it is important to consider how the strategic use of questions can promote rich whole-class discussion. Teachers pose a variety of questions to students. Some questions promote deeper mathematical thinking than others. For example, when asked "Is there another way to represent or explain your thinking?" students are given the chance to explain and justify their thinking in multiple ways. Conversely, a question like "What did you do next?" focuses only on the procedures students followed to obtain an answer. Table 2.2 is a repertoire of teacher questions linked to specific instructional goals. (See More4U for a downloadable copy.)

Table 2.2. Purposeful questions

Instructional goal: Initially eliciting students' thinking

- What did you come up with? What are you thinking?
- How did you begin working on this problem?
- How might you explain your solution?
- What have you found so far?
- What part of this problem was easy? What part was difficult?
- What do you already know about . . . ?

Probing students' answers

- How did you know?
- How did you get that answer?
- Why did you . . . ?
- How might you use a representation to show us how that works?
- Walk us through your steps. Where did you begin?
- How can you explain that in a different way?
- So, is what you're saying . . . ?

Continued on page 38

Table 2.2. (continued)

Focusing students to listen and respond to others' ideas

- What do others think about what . . . said? Do you agree or disagree? Why?
- What do you think . . . means by that?
- How does what . . . said go along with what you were thinking?
- How would you repeat what . . . just said in your own words?
- How do you think . . . got [his or her] solution?

Supporting students to make connections (e.g., between a model and a mathematical idea or specific notation)

- How is [this student's] method similar to (or different from) [that student's] method?
- What is another problem that is similar to this one?
- How is this similar to (or related to) what we learned about . . . ?
- How can we make a [picture, graph, model] of this solution?
- What part of the problem/solution does this [pointing to a particular part of a representation] represent?

Guiding students to reason mathematically (e.g., make conjectures, generalize, prove)

- How would you explain your solution?
- Does this strategy always work? Why does it work in this case?
- What do these solutions have in common?
- What math terms help us talk about this?
- What do you mean by . . . ? Can you give an explanation?
- What do you already know that could help you figure this out?
- Have we found all the possible answers?

Extending students' thinking

- What is another way to solve this problem?
- What is another situation in which we can use the same strategy to solve . . . ?
- What would happen if the numbers were changed to . . . ?

Summary and Reflection

This chapter focused on the importance of mathematical discourse in students' sense-making opportunities. Positioning students as capable and confident contributors to the formation of deep mathematics learning requires that they be active participants. Participation structures of individual engagement, small-group interactions, and whole-class discussion help students engage in meaningful dialogue. Teachers should consider their role across participation structures. We believe that student discourse is a complex, multifaceted process that results in deeper mathematical understanding. These understandings are best constructed collectively by students and facilitated by their teachers!

STRATEGIES FOR YOUR CLASSROOM

Considerations for Designing and Sustaining a Discourse-Rich Environment

Individual engagement

- Allow individual think time before sharing.

- Include visuals (e.g., representations, student strategies, and word walls) to support sense making, reasoning, and communication.

- Honor students' use of their native language.

- Explicitly teach vocabulary in conjunction with the development of concepts.

Small-group interactions

- Provide equal opportunities for all students to participate.

- Co-create norms for participation and respect at the start of the school year.

- Establish flexible groups based on students' interests, needs, and language proficiency, as well as the learning goal.

Whole-class discussions

- Model and expect students to use productive talk moves: revoicing, repeating, reasoning, building on, and wait time.

- Ask purposeful questions to probe, support, and extend student thinking.

Before you move on to the next chapter, take a moment to reflect on these questions:

STOP AND REFLECT

Pair with a colleague and reflect on your own teaching:

- What opportunities do you provide for students to engage in mathematical discourse across participation structures: individual, small group, and as a whole class?

- How do you support students' academic language development?

- What could you do to support or enhance the mathematical discourse in your classroom? What participation structures, routines, and strategies might help you achieve your learning goals?

- What comes to mind as you move beyond thinking of your class as a whole to consider supporting particular students to meaningfully engage in mathematical discourse?

Chapter 3

The Task-Rich Environment

In the course of a school day, students are asked to engage in various tasks. However, not all tasks are equally productive; different tasks lead to different levels of engagement and different learning outcomes. Traditionally, mathematics in the United States has been taught with a teaching-for-answer-getting approach: the teacher presents an algorithm and the students are given the *task* of practicing the algorithm to generate correct answers (Van de Walle, Karp, and Bay-Williams 2009). Unfortunately, this approach does not provide students with sufficient opportunities to understand or make sense of mathematics concepts and relationships, outcomes required in new standards documents and necessary for students to learn powerful mathematics.

What's needed is a greater proportion of tasks that require higher levels of student thinking, reasoning, and sense making, something Stein, Grover, and Henningsen refer to as being more "cognitively demanding" (1996, p. 461), and Norman Webb (1997) describes as having greater "depth of knowledge." Studies with mathematics learners have demonstrated that the more time students spend engaged in higher-level tasks, the greater their learning gains in both conceptual and procedural knowledge (e.g., Boaler and Staples 2008; Stein, Grover, and Henningsen 1996; Stein and Lane 1996; Stein, Remillard, and Smith 2007).

Building from the work of Mary Kay Stein, Norman Webb, and others, we refer to higher-level, cognitively demanding, deep-knowledge tasks as "juicy" tasks to convey the rich and sometimes messy nature of how these play out in the classroom. "Juicy" also suggests that student learning spills over to encompass more than a simple content objective. Mathematical knowledge is developed through real contexts, problems, situations, and models, allowing students opportunities to build more coherent, connected understandings of important concepts, relationships, and skills. Students engaged in juicy tasks develop more flexible knowledge and more diverse images of mathematics and what it means to know mathematics (Boaler and Staples 2008). When students are given time to wrestle with rich problems, find solution methods that make sense, and extend their mathematical understanding, the message to all students is, "I value your ability to think and reason and know you can figure this out." As a result, students increasingly see themselves as capable mathematical thinkers (Boaler 2015).

However, a juicy task in itself does not ensure rich learning. Researchers have noted that cognitively demanding tasks often decline in rigor during implementation (Henningsen and Stein 1997; Stein and Lane 1996). It is only when teachers carefully plan and enact lessons to allow and support students' productive struggle that a task's richness is sustained.

Unlike a rote assignment with a clear path to completion, a juicy task carries more uncertainty because it is designed to get students to think for themselves and to stretch their knowledge and understanding. This can be risky and messy—and deliciously rewarding! In the following sections, we focus on unpacking the characteristics of a juicy task and describe specific strategies teachers can use to sustain a task's potential to promote student reasoning, sense making, and deep learning.

Knowing a Juicy Task When You See One

> Mathematical tasks are used to introduce mathematical ideas and to engage and challenge students intellectually. Well-chosen tasks can pique students' curiosity and draw them into mathematics. The tasks may be connected to the real-world experiences of students, or they may arise in contexts that are purely mathematical. (National Council of Teachers of Mathematics [NCTM] 2000, pp. 18–19)

Mathematical tasks are everywhere—but not necessarily rich, juicy tasks. Consider these factors when selecting a task and when making small adjustments to strengthen the task:

- The profundity of the mathematics of the task, including the connection to important learning goals and the level of cognitive demand
- The elasticity of the task with respect to having multiple entry and exit points and forms of representation
- The relevancy of the task to students

We examine each of these characteristics in turn and base the discussion, in part, on a reflection about two tasks on the same topic (table 3.1). As you read through these, reflect on the curriculum materials you use, how well they reflect these three factors, and how you might modify them to do so even better.

Table 3.1. Two sample tasks

Task A	Task B
Find the multiplication fact families with the numbers 64, 4, and 16.	Our third-grade class is selling cupcakes for a class fund-raiser and needs to decide how to package them. The class wants to sell _____ cupcakes. What are all of the possible ways the cupcakes can be packaged if each package must have the same number of cupcakes?
	Select one of these number choices: 12 cupcakes; 24 cupcakes; 45 cupcakes. Use drawings, numbers, and words to explain your thinking and reasoning. Once you've solved the problem one way, think of a second strategy. How about a third?

STOP AND REFLECT

Spend a few minutes and solve both tasks on your own. Now, using the questions below, examine both Task A and Task B:

- Does the task allow students to closely explore and analyze important mathematics concepts, procedures, and/or reasoning strategies?

- Does the task allow multiple entry and exit points and/or multiple pathways for finding a solution?

- Does the problem connect mathematics with a situation that students may find relevant and authentic and/or with students' prior mathematical knowledge?

Profundity: Connection to mathematical learning goals and level of cognitive demand

In her 1999 book about Chinese teachers of elementary mathematics, Liping Ma referred to their focus on coherent, connected learning as developing a "profound understanding" of mathematics (Ma 1999). The concept of profundity comes from the idea that the tasks teachers use must focus attention on deep, meaningful mathematics learning goals. Drawing on research into children's learning of mathematics (National Research Council

2001), most recent standards documents feature a more coherent progression of topics both within and across grade levels. It is essential to take this coherence into account as you think about the learning goals and tasks that will guide students' day-to-day engagement with mathematics.

Task A and Task B from table 3.1 each have a mathematical focus on the relationship between factors and products. However the depth of learning promoted by Task A is limited by constraints in the numbers to be used and in what is asked of students. Students have fewer ways to engage with the mathematics and to share their mathematical thinking. Task B provides students with the opportunity to more deeply explore relationships between factors and products in the context of a relevant problem by challenging students to find all possible arrangements. The nature of the conversations generated by Task B will better support deep mathematics learning.

With a stronger focus on students' developing an understanding of the concepts behind the calculations, learning goals in today's classroom more often focus on concepts, relationships, connections, and sense making than on rote procedures and skills. What this means in terms of planning is that teachers must choose tasks that match these more rigorous goals. Mary Kay Stein and her colleagues (2009) provide a useful framework for thinking about a task's level of cognitive demand (see table 3.2, and go to More4U for a downloadable copy). Tasks with a low level of cognitive demand, such as Task A in table 3.1, are routine and straightforward and support learning goals that involve simple recall of facts or practice with already learned procedures. Although necessary to support learning, low-level cognitive demand tasks should not make up the majority of students' mathematical work. Tasks with a high level of cognitive demand, such as Task B in table 3.1, are more appropriate for learning goals involving concepts and relationships because they challenge students to reason and make connections between new knowledge and relevant prior knowledge. Such high-level tasks reflect what is to become the new normal for organizing mathematics learning in elementary classrooms.

stratford *what I want to teach like . . .*

Table 3.2. Cognitive demand and features of the task

Low-Level Cognitive Demand Tasks	High-Level Cognitive Demand Tasks
Memorization • Involves producing previously learned facts, rules, formulas, or definitions • Is routine, in that memorization involves the exact reproduction of previously learned procedures • Has no connection to related concepts	**Procedures with connections** • Focus attention on the use of procedures to develop deeper levels of understanding of mathematical concepts • Suggest general procedures that have close connections to underlying conceptual ideas • Usually are represented in multiple ways (e.g., visuals, manipulatives, symbols, problem situations) • Require engagement with the conceptual ideas that underlie the procedures to successfully complete the task
Procedures without connections • Use procedures specifically called for • Are straightforward, with little ambiguity about what needs to be done and how to do it • Are focused on producing correct answers rather than developing mathematical understanding • Require no explanations—or explanations that focus on the procedure only	**Doing mathematics** • Requires complex and non-algorithmic thinking • Requires students to explore and understand the nature of mathematical concepts, processes, or relationships • Demands self-monitoring or self-regulation of students' own cognitive processes • Requires access to relevant prior knowledge to work through the task • Requires student analysis of the task and actively examining task constraints • Requires considerable cognitive efforts

Source: Reprinted with permission from Stein et al., *Implementing Standards-Based Mathematics Instruction: A Casebook for Professional Development* (2009)

Elasticity: Multiple entry and exit points and forms of representation

A mathematical task is classified as "juicy" if it has the potential to engage students in higher-level thinking. However, students do not all learn the same thing in the same way and at the same rate. Every class at every grade level includes a range of students with varying prior experiences. Therefore, another characteristic of a juicy mathematical task is its accessibility for the diversity of learners in the classroom—it is elastic enough to stretch in different ways without losing a focus on important learning goals. Such a task is one that is challenging and accessible to all by having multiple entry and exit points. Notice that in Task B, three number choices are provided so that students can initially select a number choice that is "just right" for them. The problem also encourages the use of multiple representations and strategies. These aspects of the task were strategically designed to increase students' capacity to productively engage with the problem and to provide opportunities for students to justify, critique, and compare solution methods. Such tasks allow students to begin with a strategy that makes sense to them instead of having to use a prescribed algorithm that may or may not make sense.

Here, we offer two strategies for ensuring elasticity in task design:

- **Offer multiple number choices.** Teachers need to be mindful of the numbers that appear in the task, considering both how the values will contribute to the mathematical knowledge being developed and how students will be given access to engage productively with the task. Although not appropriate for every problem, it is often possible to provide multiple number choices for a single problem (see fig. 3.1) and allow students to select the numbers that are "just right" for them (as in Task B).

  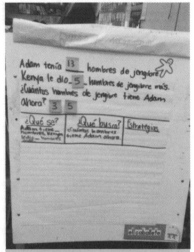

  Fig. 3.1. Word problem with number choices written in colored sticky notes

  Providing multiple number choices opens access to a wider range of learners while maintaining the cognitive demand and mathematical goals of the task. All students are able to work on the same learning goal but in ways that help them grow mathematically. The numbers a student initially selects should build on current knowledge but challenge his or her thinking (and modeling this is important so students understand the intent). For ideas on selecting the right number choices, see Tonia J. Land and colleagues' book, *Transforming the Task with Number Choice: Kindergarten through Grade 3* (2015).

- **Encourage multiple representations and strategies.** Solving a problem in two different ways or using multiple representations of a problem context increases students' capacity to solve new problems, to practice justifying their solutions, and to compare and contrast solutions. See More4U and figures 3.2 and 3.3 for two examples of problem-solving sheets that encourage students to analyze the problem context and use at least two strategies or representations when solving problems.

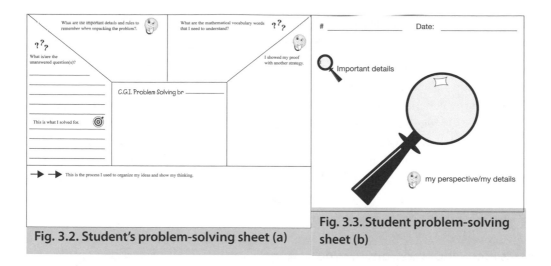

Fig. 3.2. Student's problem-solving sheet (a)

Fig. 3.3. Student problem-solving sheet (b)

Students will benefit from repeated exposure to the same representations or models. For example, when learning place value, students might use base-ten blocks to help develop understanding that successive sets of ten (powers of ten) serve as the basis for our number system. In later grades, students might use this same representation to explore concepts of multiplication through a rectangular array model. The more that students are encouraged to use the same or similar representations within and across grades, the more likely they will be to learn mathematics as connected and coherent.

Relevancy: Allow for authentic connections

A juicy task builds from students' prior knowledge and lived experiences. We often hear students in math class ask, "Why are we learning this?" Using a familiar or realistic context supports students' access to the problem by helping them make sense of the mathematics and increases engagement by providing an authentic connection of mathematics to the world around them (Civil and Andrade 2002; Foote 2011; NCTM 2014a). While Task A has no context other than the mathematical relationship among the numbers, the context of Task B is based on the scenario of a class's preparation for an upcoming fund-raiser. Having a relevant, familiar context within which to explore important mathematics gives more students access and supports learning with understanding. (In Chapter 5, we discuss strategies to design mathematical tasks that build on students' out-of-school experiences.)

Making Textbook Problems More Juicy

Most schools have published curriculum materials available, and teachers are often expected to use a particular mathematics curriculum program. All curriculum materials are written for a generic classroom and require teachers to adapt the materials to meet students' needs, strengths, and experiences. But how might typical textbook problems be modified into the juicy mathematical tasks described above? We offer a couple of ideas to get you started, and you will have many more as you become comfortable with this idea. In every case, however, be sure to use the intended learning goals as your first guide when considering how to strengthen a task; even a juicy task can be unproductive if it is not well-aligned with the learning goals.

Less is more and start from the end

Corey Drake and colleagues (2015) offer some guidance on where to find the juiciest problems in your curriculum guide. Most curriculum lessons have several components, including a warm-up activity, a variety of student tasks, differentiation suggestions, and homework. In many textbooks, the tasks that demand reasoning and problem solving are located in the textbook margins or at the end of the lesson. Making one or just a few of these tasks the focus of the lesson will enhance opportunities for reasoning and discussion while maintaining the mathematical goal of the lesson.

The key is to omit sections that *direct*, *model*, or *show* students how to solve a problem. Instead, use this time to connect the task to students' previous experiences with the mathematics topic and their out-of-school experiences (see Chapter 5 for more discussion on connecting to students' home and community-based experiences). For example, begin a lesson by asking students what they already know about this topic and how this topic has been used outside of school.

Opening up problems

A question is open when it is open-ended (multiple answers are possible) or open-middle (multiple pathways for problem solving). You might notice that this is one element of elasticity. Open questions also tend to have a higher level of cognitive demand because students need to do more than recall or follow steps in a procedure.

Open problems often allow students to approach a problem in ways that connect to their own prior knowledge. Students might be asked to find one possible solution by using both a physical/visual model and mathematical symbols. Students might also be challenged to develop a presentation and explanation of every possible solution. Another benefit of problems with multiple solutions or pathways is that they provide a rich source of material for mathematical discussion because there are bound to be several ways in which students approach them.

STOP AND REFLECT

Before reading further, consider how you can modify Task A, to find the multiplication fact families with the numbers of 64, 4, and 16, so it is a juicier problem.

Table 3.3 suggests some strategies to modify the closed problem "Find the multiplication fact families with the numbers of 64, 4, and 16" into juicier open questions.

Table 3.3. Examples to open up the fact family closed problem

Strategy	Open Question Example
Strategy 1: Give the answer and ask for the problem.	The solution to an equation is 64. What's the equation? Create a story problem to represent the equation $4 \times 16 = 64$.
Strategy 2: Take out an element of the problem.	Make this true in as many ways as you can. $64 = \underline{} \times \underline{}$ What is a possible perimeter for a rectangle with an area of 64? Can you think of another? A third?
Strategy 3: Offer two situations or examples, and ask for similarities and differences.	How is multiplication like division? How is it different? How is multiplying numbers like adding them? How is it different?

Source: Small (2009)

Implementing Juicy Tasks

Juicy tasks that give students opportunities to refine and extend their mathematical understanding through processes of reasoning and sense making are difficult to implement well as they lack a specific, obvious solution path (Henningsen and Stein 1997; Stein, Grover, and Henningsen 1996; Stein and Lane 1996). This is intentional because it is students' productive struggle with trying out various pathways that will lead to deep learning. When your students are wrestling with the mathematics, you may feel the urge to step in and lead them to a specific solution path; however, this would reduce the cognitive demand from high level to low level, and it would short-circuit students' growth toward rigorous learning goals. As teachers ourselves, we understand this urge to step in and have caught ourselves doing so more often than we'd like to admit. But it is important to resist this urge and instead use strategies that guide students' reasoning and sense making, helping them learn to persevere.

For the remainder of this chapter, we offer guidance on how to scaffold students' problem solving while maintaining the cognitive demand of a juicy task throughout its implementation. Task implementation is often described as having three stages: launch, student exploration, and discussion of strategies. However, possibly the most critical stage is what we do *before* the implementation of the task—the planning. Therefore, our discussion of implementation includes four stages: planning, launching, supporting student exploration, and guiding discussion. We illustrate these four stages through a problem that examines the mathematical reasoning behind students' strategies for multiplication as a means to refine their understanding of properties of arithmetic.

STOP AND REFLECT

Before reading further, try to solve this problem:

Maya's mother is making a patchwork quilt. She wants to make a rectangular quilt that is 8 ft by 17 ft. If each square for the patchwork is 1 ft by1 ft, how many squares are needed?

Maya finds the area of the quilt in the following way:

$$8 \times 17 = (5 + 3) \times 17$$
$$= 5 \times (3 + 17)$$
$$= 5 \times 20$$

1. Do you agree with Maya's reasoning? Why or why not? Use pictures, numbers, and words to defend your thinking.

2. Find another way to calculate the area of the rectangular quilt. Explain why your method is correct.

We chose to illustrate the stages of a lesson with the quilt problem for several reasons. The problem is challenging and requires students to engage in sense making and reasoning around multiplication and area. Multiplication is a critical topic in third grade. Students need to develop an understanding of the meaning of multiplication of whole numbers within varied contexts—equal-sized groups, arrays, and area models—and they must learn to use properties of arithmetic when making sense of algorithms and when solving for unknown factors. The quilt problem provides a context for students to examine varied representations of multiplication and strategies for multiplying whole numbers.

The task asks students to critique the reasoning of others and to analyze a progression of statements to explore the truth of a conjecture. In this case, students investigate the reasoning of a student who has attempted to extend understanding of the properties of addition to work with multiplication. Since addition has the property of being both commutative and associative, addends can be decomposed, reordered, and regrouped while maintaining equivalence, as in the example below:

$$\begin{aligned} 8 + 17 &= (5 + 3) + 17 \\ &= 5 + (3 + 17) \\ &= 5 + 20 \end{aligned}$$

Students who are beginning to learn about the operation of multiplication (as well as those with an incomplete conceptual understanding of multiplication) will often try to apply similar reasoning when working with factors, not yet having learned to make sense of the distributive property. This is what we see with Maya's work:

$$\begin{aligned} 8 \times 17 &= (5 + 3) \times 17 \\ &= 5 \times (3 + 17) \\ &= 5 \times 20 \end{aligned}$$

This task is meant to give students the opportunity to explore the operation of multiplication and to begin to articulate an understanding of the distributive property. At third grade, students do not need to use the formal terminology for these properties but are developing an understanding that properties are rules about how numbers work. Let's begin our examination of the quilt problem with a discussion of the lesson planning.

Setting Instructional Goals

It's important to consider the first component of the work of teaching a lesson—planning. A critical starting point for planning is to identify clear, profound learning goals with attention given to the level of cognitive demand required. What are students to know and understand about mathematics as a result of their engagement in the lesson?

The lesson learning goal can be stated in a variety of ways, reflecting different levels of specificity, as shown in the chart in table 3.4. Goal A and Goal B indicate what students are expected to do during the lesson, but they do not provide insight into the mathematical understanding that students should develop. In contrast, Goal C is more specific about what students will learn and focuses on developing students' capacity to analyze and critique other students' reasoning around the properties of addition and multiplication. Students will need to reason inductively about Maya's strategy, distinguishing the correct application or reasoning of the properties from that which is incorrect and explaining why, using physical or visual models or symbols and words. The specificity of the learning goal guides the decision making about task selection and implementation to better capitalize on opportunities to advance students' learning.

Table 3.4. Three learning goals for the patchwork quilt problem

Goal A: Students will find the number of square units of a rectangular patchwork quilt that is 8 ft by 17 ft.

Goal B: Students will be able to use multiplication to find the number of square units of a rectangular patchwork quilt that is 8 ft by 17 ft.

Goal C: Students will evaluate and apply strategies for multiplication that demonstrate an understanding of the distributive property.

We will now explore instructional episodes in which two third-grade teachers use the quilt task as the basis for a lesson in which students investigate the properties of multiplication, in particular the distributive property, and consider its use to solve more complex multiplication problems. We will consider how the lesson's learning goal guided the teachers' decision making and the ways in which the teachers maintained the cognitive rigor of the task throughout implementation.

TEACHING TIP: USING QUICK IMAGES

Lisa So uses "quick images" of real-life contexts to begin students' investigation of multiplication. The use of real-life contexts encourages students to examine grouping structures used in our daily context (e.g., postage stamps, windows in city buildings, fruits and vegetables arranged in bins, bakers' trays). "Quick image" refers to how the image is presented and discussed. The image is flashed for two or three seconds so students cannot rely on counting by ones and will instead see objects in groups (and as groups of groups). Invite students to share how they "saw the stamps." For example, students may figure out the amount of stamps in the image in figure 3.4 as 4 rows with 6 in each row, 4 groups of 3 twice, or 4 groups of 5 plus another 4.

Fig. 3.4. Stamps quick image

A Peek Inside a Classroom: The Task Launch

What follows is a transcript of Mrs. So's five-minute launch of the patchwork quilt task:

[*Mrs. So begins with a PowerPoint that poses the problem displayed on the board:*]

Mrs. So: Today, for our math exploration, we're going to help solve a problem for Maya's family. Maya's mother is making a patchwork quilt. She wants to make a rectangular quilt that is 8 ft by 17 ft. If each square for the quilt is 1 ft by 1 ft, how many squares are needed? Let's think about the information presented. As a reader, one of our strategies is visualization. As we visualize, we're making a mental picture in our head. What mental image shows up as you read this problem? What is the picture in your head, Manola?

Manola: The picture in my head is a quilt, 8 ft by 17 ft long with squares 1 ft by 1 ft.

Mrs. So: Manola, you have an image of a patchwork quilt. Class, show me *shakas* [*class hand signal for when students agree with another student's response*] if you also have a picture of a patchwork quilt in your head.

[*Mrs. So shows the next slide of her PowerPoint (fig. 3.5). The image of a patchwork quilt appears on the monitor.*]

Mrs. So: Remember the last story we just read, *The Keeping Quilt*?

Fig. 3.5. Patchwork quilt image

[*The class is currently engaged in an interdisciplinary project-based unit of study on family heritage. The Keeping Quilt by Patricia Polacco is about a family creating a quilt out of pieces of material from clothes worn by family members.*]

Mrs. So: That was what I was thinking. Here's the patchwork quilt, just like in our story. What do you notice about the quilt?

William: Lots of colors.

Mrs. So:	Anything else? Any other observations?
Emy:	There's row and columns with 17 squares.
Mrs. So:	We have rows and columns that are 17 ft long. Manola, you had said earlier that they were 1 ft by 1 ft squares. Anything anyone would like to add to that? Any wonderings about the squares themselves?
Felix:	It's an array.
Mrs. So:	It's an array. What does that mean?
Felix:	It's objects put together in rows and columns.
Mrs. So:	Anyone want to add to that?
Sienna:	An array shows you something in rows and columns. This quilt can be 8 down and 17 across or 17 down and 8 across.
Mrs. So:	We see rows and columns with squares in each row and column. So, what are we trying to figure out?
Olivia:	We're trying to figure out how many squares are there.
Mrs. So:	When we're trying to figure out how many squares there are, what are we trying to figure out?
Deanne:	We're trying to figure out the area.
Mrs. So:	What is area?
Deanne:	It's the inside. It's not the perimeter. It's the inside of it.
Mrs. So:	When we talk about area, we're talking about the amount of space covering a region. In this case, Olivia said we're talking about how many squares cover up the quilt. These are all important observations. Today, our job is to help Maya figure out how many of these squares are needed to make the patchwork quilt. Think a bit about how you might go about figuring this out in your head.

[*Mrs. So gives the students a minute to think on their own. Then, Mrs. So displays Maya's solution on the screen:*

$$8 \times 17 = (5 + 3) \times 17$$
$$= 5 \times (3 + 17)$$
$$= 5 \times 20]$$

| Mrs. So: | Here's Maya's strategy to figure out the number of quilt squares on the patchwork quilt. Explain Maya's strategy to your neighbor. Explain her strategy in your own words. |

[*During two minutes of pair talk, Mrs. So walks around listening to group conversations.*]

Analyzing the launch

Mrs. So's class has just finished their unit on addition and subtraction in which the instructional focus was on developing understanding and fluency in solving multi-digit arithmetic based on place-value understanding and the properties of operations. As a significant part of this development, students spent time putting numbers together and taking them apart in a variety of ways. Students explored their own and others' invented methods of addition and subtraction. The class has just started an exploration of multiplication and has spent the last week engaging in activities with various representations of multiplication involving equal-sized groups, arrays, and area models through the use of quick images and conceptual cards (figs. 3.6 and 3.7). These activities were meant to develop students' understanding of multiplication through exploration of number relationships and grouping strategies based on extending properties of addition to their work with multiplication.

TEACHING TIP: USING CONCEPTUAL FLASHCARDS

Conceptual flashcards develop reasoning strategies and facility with basic facts as students use number relationships to visualize and solve the facts. Unlike traditional basic fact flashcards, conceptual flashcards help students determine and illustrate their own strategy, using known facts to solve an unknown fact.

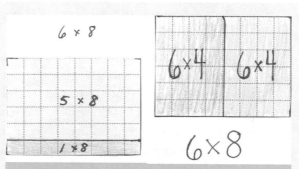

Figs. 3.6 and 3.7. Student-created conceptual flashcards; Source: Bray (2014), p. 400

Mrs. So's goal in using the patchwork quilt task was to support her students' growing understanding of the use of the properties of arithmetic as a strategy: using products they know to solve products they don't know. In addition, many of her students were incorrectly applying the associative and commutative properties of addition to solve multiplication problems, not having developed an understanding of the distributive property. The assignment was intentionally designed to examine these common errors and allow students to refine and extend understanding of the operation of multiplication.

The focus of Mrs. So's launch was to ensure that students understood the various aspects of the problem well enough to get started. Let's consider three critical elements of the task launch (Jackson et al. 2012):

1. **Discuss the key mathematical idea.** Focusing solely on context is not enough. It is also critical to discuss the key mathematical ideas without hinting at particular strategies to solve the task. The patchwork quilt problem requires students to realize that the quilt consists of many squares of the same size organized in rows with a set number of squares in each row. The squares cover the "area" of the quilt—the measure of the space covering the surface of the quilt. Mrs. So provokes this discussion by asking students what they notice about the squares on the quilt. This is an intentional move. Mrs. So is focusing on clarity; she wants to make sure that everyone is clear on the key mathematical ideas under investigation.

2. **Develop common language to describe the key features.** Another launch focus is to both support and press students to develop common language to describe any feature of the task—contextual features, mathematical ideas, and any other language—that might be unfamiliar or confusing. Mrs. So anticipated that the words "patchwork quilt," "squares," and "area" needed to be explained, and she did so by allowing students to use their own words during the setup.

3. **Maintain the cognitive demand.** To maintain the mathematical rigor of the task, teachers must avoid suggesting a particular solution method. Doing so takes away students' opportunity to develop their mathematical understanding as they generate their own solution methods and representations, Mrs. So maintained the rigor by helping students understand the key aspects of the task while leaving solution pathways open. The PowerPoint slides used in this task are available as More4U resources.

Exploration

The exploration phase starts as soon as the students begin to work on the task and continues until the teacher and students convene to wrap up the lesson. In their analysis of hundreds of classroom lessons, Stein and colleagues (1996) found that the exploration phase was the most important influence on what students actually learn. Both the teacher and the students are important contributors to how the task is carried out. High-level tasks

TEACHING TIP: USING THE BET LINE

The bet line, a prediction strategy for reading, is another way to engage students in decoding the context of a task given as a word problem. Here's how the bet line works:

1. **Introduce the first line of the word problem.** Allow students to discuss what they know so far.

2. **Ask, "What do you bet will happen next?"** Have students predict the next part of the word problem.

3. **Show the next line of the word problem.** Then, once again, discuss what they know so far and what they bet the question will ask them.

4. **Reveal the actual question posed.** Many students will have already beaten you to the punch . . . and started thinking about strategies to figure it out!

See More4U for a video clip of Ruth Freedman-Finch using the bet line strategy. More information on the bet line strategy can be found in the article by Lara Dick and colleagues, "Supporting Sense Making with Mathematical Bet Lines" (2016) (http://www.nctm.org/Publications /Teaching-Children-Mathematics/2016/Vol22/Issue9/Supporting-Sense -Making-with-Mathematical-Bet-Lines/).

(such as the quilt problem) tend to be less structured and more difficult, and they tend to take a longer time to solve than the kinds of tasks students are typically exposed to. Discomfort often comes with this uncertainty, and, in order to deal with their discomfort, students may ask for more explicit guidelines on how to break up the problem into smaller steps or for a specific procedure to solve the problem (Stein, Grover, and Henningsen 1996). It is in response to these requests that teachers often give in, and the challenging, reasoning aspects of the task are reduced.

Stein and colleagues (1996) offer some guidance on how to maintain the rigor and opportunity for students to reason and problem-solve during the exploration stage. Let's look at these points in connection with the exploration stage of Mrs. Freedman-Finch's implementation of the patchwork quilt lesson with her third-grade class:

1. Students need sufficient time (not too little and not too much) to explore the task. They need time to wrestle with the demanding aspects, but too much time may allow them to drift into off-task behavior.

As students work on the patchwork quilt task, Mrs. Freedman-Finch circulates around the room, observing and annotating their approach to the problem. She notices that many of the students are justifying their reasoning through their own examples. They are solving the problem "8 × 17" in multiple ways, with the majority using two or more strategies: drawing an array or area model, using repeated addition and place-value understanding to figure out the answer. However, only a few critique the reasoning in Maya's strategy.

Instead of intervening, Mrs. Freedman-Finch lets them work for a short time more. After 10 minutes of exploration, she asks student groups to convene for a "conference period" to discuss their mathematical thinking. At this time, students are asked to explain their current thinking and reasoning and to pose their questions and concerns to the others.

2. Press for justifications, explanations, and meaning.

Mrs. Freedman-Finch sets up one or two conference periods strategically throughout the exploration stage. These conference periods (fig. 3.8) are used to hold students accountable for explanations and justifications throughout the implementation stage. Research tells us that students' learning deepens when they are encouraged to become the

Fig. 3.8. Student math conference

authors of their own ideas and when they are held accountable for reasoning about and understanding key concepts (Engle and Conant 2002).

Mrs. Freedman-Finch starts the conferencing with the prompt:

> Explain to the other group members how you reasoned about Maya's strategy. The listening group, be prepared to explain your colleagues' reasoning. If their ideas are not clear to you or you have questions or disagreements, make sure you discuss this. This is an opportunity to support each other. Make good use of your time.

Students are instructed to reflect, explain, and justify their sense making to others, and they are held accountable for actively listening, critiquing, and understanding the reasoning of others. Students experience a sustained press for justification, explanation, and meaning throughout implementation, not just from Mrs. Freedman-Finch as she walks around the room but from each other as well.

3. Monitor and reflect on their problem-solving process.
The conference periods also provide frequent opportunities for students to monitor and reflect on their process of mathematical problem solving. Productive problem solvers periodically take stock of their progress to see whether they seem to be on the right track (Bransford, Brown, and Cocking 2000; Schoenfeld 1987).

Mrs. Freedman-Finch has found that as students are explaining their thinking to peers, they are self-assessing their progress and often catch their own mistakes and adjust their strategies accordingly.

4. Scaffold student thinking and reasoning through questioning. The type of scaffolding provided is critical. Teachers need to provide just enough support to keep thinking in motion without simplifying the problem. Often in our work with teachers, we are asked what the key questions should be. No perfect question or set of questions exists that would work for all students and all problems. What really matters is not what teachers *say* but how well they *listen* to students' thinking in order to comprehend how they are understanding the mathematics.

TEACHING TIP: PARTNER SHARE

How can teachers quickly partner students beyond working with just the neighboring student? Desiree Olivas uses the clock buddies strategy to create mixed-abilities pairs for partnered activities. Students are given a clock handout (fig. 3.9) and asked to "make appointments" with each other to fill up their clock. Buddies can be used for many purposes (revisit Chapter 2 for examples of how to align student grouping strategies with learning goals), and they are particularly helpful for a quick share-and-reflect during task exploration. A blank clock handout is available at More4U.

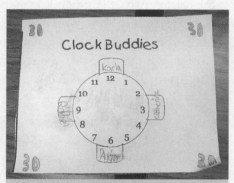

Fig. 3.9. Student clock buddies sheet

The follow-up teacher moves should serve to direct students' attention to closely examining the problem, considering the organization of available diagrams, and expressing their mathematical thinking in words and symbols. Below is a list of questions that Dr. Olivas, who also assigned the quilt task to her students, used to orient students to the details of Maya's reasoning and to press them to ground their arguments in concrete referents, such as objects, drawings, diagrams, words, and equations.

- Do you agree or disagree with Maya's reasoning? Why? Can you prove it?

- What was Maya doing? What was Maya trying to do?

- Why do you disagree with Maya? What specifically do you disagree with?

- Where do you think she went wrong? What would you say if you could talk to her? What should she have done?

Discussion

A whole-class discussion is essential to bring some mathematical closure to the thinking students have been doing. In this stage, students collectively engage in "accountable talk"—discussing, justifying, and challenging various solutions to the problem that all have just worked on (Chapin, O'Connor, and Anderson 2009). The discussion is when much of the deep learning takes place as students reflect individually and collectively on the ideas they have explored.

The teacher plays a critical role in guiding the discussion. Teachers make discussions productive when they know what questions to pose; strategically select and sequence specific students to share; and ask questions to illuminate connections across strategies, ideas, and concepts. At the center of a productive discussion is making purposeful decisions based on the mathematical goals of the lesson.

FOUR REASONS TO END MATH LESSONS WITH A WHOLE-CLASS DISCUSSION

- Talk can reveal what students understand—and what they don't understand *yet*.

- Hearing and talking about concepts, procedures, and applications boost memory.

- Students can gain a deeper understanding of mathematical concepts as they share their reasoning—and critique others' reasoning.

- Talking supports language development. When it's used extensively, students get a richer sense of what words and phrases mean and when to use them.

Types of strategy share

In Chapter 2, we discussed the development of norms for whole-class discussion, the selection of strategies for sharing, and how to ask purposeful questions. Here, we build on these and examine how these decisions are determined in relation to the mathematical goal of the lesson. The mathematical goal acts as a compass to navigate classroom talk and helps decide what to listen for, which ideas to pursue, and what to highlight.

Open strategy share

Elham Kazemi and Allison Hintz (2014) call the most common form of group discussion "open strategy share." In an open strategy share, the goal is to build students' repertoire of strategies and to show that there are different ways of thinking about the same problem. A guiding question is "Did you solve it a different way?" or "What's another way to solve this problem?" Lots of ideas are generated, and the discussion is likely to move across a broad landscape of mathematical concepts, procedures, representations, and explanations.

The teacher's role is to bring out a range of possible ways to solve the same problem and to help students make sense of each other's strategies. Teacher questions focus on HOWs, such as "How did _____ solve the problem? How is this problem similar to (or related to) the stamp problem from last week?" and WHYs, such as "Why did you break up 8 into 4 and 4? Why did _____ decide to break apart 17 into 10 and 7?"

Targeted strategy share

Open strategy share is just one form of discussion. The type of student discourse that leads to richer mathematical learning—comparing and contrasting ideas and strategies; reasoning and proof of one's idea and those of others; or applying a strategy, tool, or error analysis—often does not occur just by chance but has been intentionally planned. Kazemi and Hintz (2014) call discussions with a specific focus "targeted sharing."

At More4U, you will find video excerpts of classroom discussions of the patchwork quilt task from two different classrooms. Although the two third-grade classrooms engaged in the same math task, each classroom discussion had a different instructional goal and was led differently. The table below highlights the targeted discussion structures in the two classrooms.

Table 3.5. Discussion structure, discussion goal, and teacher questions for two classrooms

Teacher	Targeted Discussion Structure	Discussion Goal	Teacher Questions
Mrs. So	Compare and contrast	The discussion compares similarities and differences among strategies.	• What are some commonalities, similarities, and parallels between these two models? • How are they both arrays? • What do you notice about the differences between these two students' models? • When would it be a good time to use one model? When would it be a good time to use the other?

Table 3.5 (*continued*)

Mrs. Freedman-Finch	Why? Let's justify.	The discussion zooms in on one strategy, with a focus on making sense of and justifying the reasoning behind the strategy.	• Explain Maya's strategy in your own words. What did she do? • What are you thinking about with Maya's strategy? • You said the first equation is different from the second equation? How?

As you watch the two videos, consider the following questions to guide your viewing:

• What do you notice about what the teacher and the students are doing? What type of discussion is it?

• How does the teacher support students so they know what to share? How does the teacher make sure that students' ideas are heard and are useful to others?

• How does the teacher orient students to one another—and the mathematical concepts being covered—so that every member of the class is involved in achieving the mathematical goal?

• How does the teacher communicate that all student ideas are valued?

Summary and Reflection

Juicy tasks demand critical thinking, encourage conceptual understanding, and provide students with opportunities to develop mathematical habits of mind. Such tasks are built around profound learning goals, are cognitively challenging, have multiple entry points, invite the use of multiple representations and multiple solution paths, and engage students' interests. From the task launch to its culmination, students play an active, central role in exploring, solving, and sharing. The teacher's role is to provide an environment for risk-taking, to see mistakes as a means to further learning, and to allow varied opportunities for students to reflect and explain their thinking with their learning community.

STRATEGIES FOR YOUR CLASSROOM

Considerations for Designing a Task-Rich Environment

Lesson planning

- Select juicy tasks that are mathematically and cognitively challenging, have multiple entry points and solution paths, and build from students' lived experiences.

- Make sure that tasks are designed to support students in meeting the learning goal of the lesson.

Launch

- Identify the context of the problem to discuss any potentially unfamiliar features.

- Discuss the key mathematical ideas without hinting at particular strategies to solve the task.

- Develop common language to describe any feature of the task—contextual features, mathematical ideas, and any other words that might be unfamiliar or confusing.

Exploration

- Give sufficient time for students to wrestle with the demands of the task.

- Press students to explain and justify their thinking.

- Allow frequent opportunities for students to monitor and reflect on their problem-solving process.

- Scaffold student thinking and reasoning through questioning.

Discussion

- Focus the discussion on the sharing of student thinking, formalizing the main ideas of the lesson, and highlighting connections among strategies and to prior learning.

- Make purposeful decisions on the basis of the mathematical goals for the math talk.

STOP AND REFLECT

Pair with your grade-level team or a colleague, and videotape your teaching. As you observe and reflect on your videotaped lesson, consider the following questions:

- What type of task are students engaged in? Is the task mathematically/ cognitively challenging? Does it have multiple entry points and solution paths? Does it build from students' life experiences? What could you do to make the task juicier?

- How did you scaffold students' problem solving while maintaining the cognitive demand of the task during the launch and exploration? What are the strengths and weaknesses in your current task launch and exploration? What would you modify? Why?

- Describe the kinds of communication that take place during your classroom discussion. What is the discussion type? What is the discussion goal?

Chapter 4

The Assessment-Rich Environment

When teachers, students, and parents think about assessment, what often comes to mind are tests and quizzes and how these are used to assign grades and label students' progress or achievement. They might also think of students' anxiety about test-taking and the high-stakes nature of some assessments. This popular notion of assessment as evaluation neglects the more important aspect of assessment as a method of generating information (data) that informs learning and instruction. Education researcher Dylan Wiliam explains why the formative use of assessment data is so powerful:

> An assessment functions formatively to the extent that evidence about student achievement is elicited, interpreted, and used by teachers, learners, or their peers to make decisions about the next steps in instruction that are likely to be better than the decisions they would have made in the absence of that evidence. (2011, p. 43)

Similarly, the National Council of Teachers of Mathematics (NCTM) describes assessment as "a process whose primary purpose is to gather data that support the teaching and learning of mathematics" (2014a, p. 89).

It might help to consider the generating of data as only one part of a larger process of assessment: collecting data from student responses and work related to specific learning goals, interpreting what the data say about students' progress toward learning goals, and acting on this to further students' learning (see fig. 4.1). More important, it is not only the teacher who can engage in interpreting assessment data and guiding future actions; it is even more powerful when students develop the habit of doing so, both as peer assessment and as self-assessment. No matter who is involved, how data are used to improve learning and instruction makes all the difference!

Fig. 4.1. Process of assessment chart

This process of assessment to inform teaching and further learning has been shown to lead to significant improvements in academic outcomes for students (Black and Wiliam 1998; Hattie 2012). In fact, as Ernest points out, "Without teacher or peer correction, i.e., formal or informal assessment and feedback, learners will not have their conceptions and actions 'shaped,' and cannot know that they are mastering the intended mathematical content correctly" (1999, p. 79).

The vision for mathematical learning that drives new standards emphasizes students' understanding of mathematical concepts and relationships, students' application of mathematics to meaningful contexts, and students' engagement in practices of reasoning and sense making with mathematics. Although procedural knowledge and facts contribute to this vision, they play only a supporting role. As such, assessment in mathematics must reflect this vision by including a wide range of mathematical knowledge and practices beyond procedures alone.

This chapter explores ideas for assessing mathematical knowledge (conceptual, procedural, and factual/notational) and mathematical practices (e.g., reasoning, justification, problem solving). These types of knowledge will be described and explored later in this chapter. Before reading ahead, examine the following reflection prompts, and consider how you might strengthen any areas for which you are not satisfied with your response.

Articulating Clear Learning Goals

Being intentional about the use of assessment requires understanding not only the specific learning goals for a given instructional sequence but also how these goals fit into a larger learning progression, including prerequisite knowledge and connections to other mathematical concepts and later learning. This perspective allows you—and your students—to see their knowledge as developmental, a point along a learning progression, rather than as discrete topics students simply "know" or "don't know." Many recent standards documents are organized to support more coherent learning of mathematics. Detailed information about learning progressions—descriptions of how key mathematical "big ideas" (Charles 2005) build along a continuum and schematics showing interconnections among concepts and skills—may be found in state or provincial standards documents as well as in curriculum guides. Achieve, a nonprofit reform organization, helped develop the Common Core State Standards and Next Generation Science Standards and created The Coherence Map website, http://achievethecore.org/coherence-map/, to illustrate the structure of and connections within the *Common Core State Standards for Mathematics* (National Governors Association Center for Best Practices and Council of Chief State School Officers [NGA Center and CCSSO] 2010). Having knowledge of the connections and relationships between mathematical concepts allows teachers to design more meaningful and informative assessments (Charles 2005).

The starting point for all formative assessment is a clearly articulated learning goal and an understanding of how this goal fits into a learning progression. Once you know the desired student outcomes, you can have a better understanding of how to design checkpoints throughout a lesson and unit to gauge students' progress and to inform your instructional decision making. Mathematics learning goals can be categorized as conceptual knowledge, factual and notational knowledge, procedural knowledge, and knowledge of mathematical practices. Note that in this chapter we use the Standards for Mathematical Practice (MPs) from the *Common Core State Standards for Mathematics* (NGA Center and CCSSO 2010) as the "mathematical practices" knowledge. These are derived in large part from NCTM's Process Standards (NCTM 2000) and *Adding It Up* (National Research Council 2001) and are likely to be similar to the mathematical practices in other sets of standards.

Table 4.1 gives descriptors and examples for each of these types of mathematical knowledge. Although we list them separately, the various types of knowledge are interrelated and mutually supportive. For instance, in developing understanding of procedural knowledge for adding two decimal fractions (see the Deepening Mathematics Knowledge text box for a discussion of this term), students draw on their knowledge of the concept of decimal fractions, the procedure of addition, and the notation for decimals. Indeed, research has shown a bidirectional relationship in particular among conceptual and procedural knowledge in mathematics (Rittle-Johnson, Schneider, and Star 2015).

DEEPENING MATHEMATICS KNOWLEDGE

Many of us learned mathematics through rote memorization and mimicry of procedures with little attention given to underlying concepts or relationships. For this reason, as teachers, we authors have had to take time to revisit mathematical topics and build an understanding of the concepts behind the calculations.

One example is the concept of decimal fractions (more commonly referred to as "decimals"). When students learn decimals only as an extension of the base-ten place-value system, they do not connect decimals to fraction notation. For instance, when presented with 0.005, students might read it as "point zero, zero, five" and know that this is less than a whole. But this is of limited value, compared with being able to recognize 0.005 as "five thousandths" and as equivalent to $5/1000$. Understanding that decimals are simply fractions with a denominator that is a power of 10 empowers students to make connections with fraction understanding and to better understand arithmetic operations with decimals. For books aimed at deepening teachers' mathematical knowledge, see NCTM's *Developing Essential Understanding of . . .* series.

Table 4.1. Types of mathematical knowledge

Knowledge	Descriptors	Examples
Conceptual	Classifications, relationships, generalizations, principles, structures	What are decimal fractions, and how are they distinguished from other fractions?
Factual and notational	Facts, symbols, notation	How do you write three and one-tenth as a decimal? What is the place value of the 5 in 0.125?
Procedural	Algorithms, methods, operations	How do you add two decimals? What method is most efficient for finding 30 percent of 75?
Mathematical practices	Habits, strategies, dispositions	In a problem such as finding the cost of 38 pizzas for a school fund-raiser if each pizza is $11.79, ask students to explain how their mathematical work or visual representations relate to the original context. This assesses the practice of reasoning abstractly and quantitatively.

Sources: Anderson and Krathwohl (2001); Hiebert (1986); NGA Center and CCSSO (2010); U.S. Department of Education (2003)

Let's take an example and see what this might look like in practice. The following is a fifth-grade standard in the *Common Core State Standards for Mathematics* (NGA Center and CCSSO 2010; 5.NBT.A.3): "Read, write, and compare decimals to thousandths." As we think about the knowledge required to demonstrate mastery of this standard and how it fits within a larger learning progression, we might include the following:

- Explaining the relationship between decimals and whole numbers (conceptual)
- Explaining the relationship between decimal notation and fraction notation (conceptual and notational)
- Reading and writing place-value notation and names for decimals (factual and notational)
- Forming equivalent decimals and equivalent fractions (procedural and conceptual)
- Comparing decimals and fractions (procedural and conceptual)
- Recognizing that working with decimals requires precise use of language and notation (mathematical practice and notational)

In the sections that follow, we offer suggestions for assessing each type of mathematical knowledge (conceptual, procedural, and factual/notational) and mathematical practices (e.g., reasoning, justification, problem solving).

A Peek Inside a Classroom

We highlight an instructional episode from Mayra Orozco's fifth-grade class to provide context for our discussion of assessments:

Mrs. Orozco is working with her dual-language (English/Spanish) class to develop an understanding of decimal place value and operations with decimals. Her students spent a couple of days with decimal place value earlier in the year. As they begin a unit on arithmetic operations with decimals in December, Mrs. Orozco wants to gauge their understanding of the decimal fraction concept and their fluency with positional notation, place-value notation. She uses a card sort activity (see the description later in this chapter) with student pairs as a way to remind them of prior learning and to bring to the surface any alternative conceptions that can inform her instructional decision making (see the Alternative Conceptions box for a discussion of this term.) Students are asked to cut out the cards and sort or order them in any way that they can explain mathematically. As students are working on their sorts, Mrs. Orozco circulates and probes their thinking with questions such as "Why did you place these two numbers here?" and "How do you know which of these two decimals is larger?" and "What if there were a zero placed at the end of this decimal number?"

ALTERNATIVE CONCEPTIONS

Our use of "alternative conceptions" rather than the more common "misconceptions" reflects a belief that students' errors are grounded in *some conception* that is different from what is deemed correct within the discipline of mathematics. Understanding how students are thinking, especially when they are making errors, provides a basis for deciding how best to provoke further thinking and a revised conception. In this way, learning is not about replacing misconceptions but about revising, reorganizing, refining, and building on from current conceptions and prior understandings (see J. Smith, diSessa, and Roschelle 1993).

Partners prompt one another to take out a sheet with place-value names from their earlier lessons and help each other with the Spanish names for the decimal places (see More4U for a downloadable copy of the chart). They also have discussions about the correct ordering of the numbers, reminding each other of relationships between whole units, tenths, hundredths, and thousandths.

After ten minutes of pair work, Mrs. Orozco has noticed several alternative conceptions around the meaning of decimal place values and the role of zero in decimal fractions, with many students unsure of the difference between 0.25 and 0.025 or claiming that 2.804 is equivalent to 2.84. With her tablet, she takes a photo of one pair's sorted cards to project on the front board for the class to use as a point of discussion on place-value names and meanings (see fig. 4.2). After the lesson, Mrs. Orozco decides

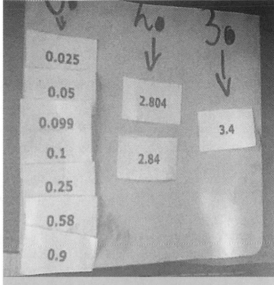

Fig. 4.2. Photo of one student pair's card sort

that her students will benefit from one more lesson focused on understanding the concept of decimal numbers, with a specific focus on tenths and hundredths using multiple representations. Using ideas from her textbook as well as from colleagues at her site, she plans a follow-up lesson. Students will use coins and bills, base-ten blocks, written numerals, and hundredths grids (a hundred grid renamed to represent one whole in hundredths) to represent several quantities of money she will read to them in the context of a story.

Assessment of Conceptual Knowledge

We start with a focus on conceptual knowledge because all of the work that is done in a mathematics classroom should be grounded in students' understanding of mathematical relationships, principles, and structures. As NCTM states, "Effective teaching of mathematics builds fluency with procedures on a foundation of conceptual understanding" (2014a, p. 10). Let's examine one definition of conceptual knowledge. Hiebert and Lefevre describe conceptual knowledge as established in relation to prior knowledge and other concepts:

> [Conceptual knowledge] can be thought of as a connected web of knowledge, a network in which linking relationships are as prominent as the discrete pieces of information.

Relations pervade the individual facts and propositions so that all pieces of information are linked to some network. (1986, pp. 3–4)

There are three essential characteristics of assessments for conceptual knowledge:

1. Focus on "why" questions to examine students' reasoning and sense making.
2. Probe common alternative conceptions.
3. Emphasize student discourse (written or verbal) about connections between multiple representations or relationships between mathematical objects.

In order for assessments to support the development of conceptual knowledge, they must be designed to elicit students' thinking about specific concepts and relationships for self, peers, and teacher to examine. Once elicited, students' conceptions can be discussed, examined, challenged, and ultimately refined or extended. We see this in Mrs. Orozco's card sort decimal representation activities where students had to justify their reasoning and represent their thinking visually. These processes of justification and representation helped many students realize some of their conceptions about decimal numbers had to be revised. We want to acknowledge that assessing for conceptual knowledge requires teachers to have deep understanding of mathematics concepts. Each of us has stories about "aha" moments in our own teaching when our understanding was challenged and deepened by listening to a student's explanation. While teachers' conceptions of mathematics are more advanced than those of their students, this does not mean that there is no room for further revisions and refinements.

What follows are examples of assessment strategies that are designed to get at students' knowledge of concepts in ways that reflect the three characteristics above. As you read each activity, consider the sort of thinking that is required of students, how students' responses provide insight into their understandings, and what sort of feedback you might provide, both to inform students' in-the-moment learning and to guide future learning.

Card sort

Best used in pairs or small groups, card sorts ask students to separate a set of cards into specific categories as a way to examine their understanding of concept and relationship. Mrs. Orozco's class used the set of cards in figure 4.3 (see More4U for downloadable card sets and a card set template). For any card sort, consider asking students to categorize them in two ways. First, students sort items into self-selected categories (not more than three) on the basis of how they feel the items should be organized and by their relationship to each other. Second, ask students to sort by numerical value to assess their sense for the relative size of the number. For example, the card set in figure 4.3 can be sorted into three groups—less than one-half, more than one-half, and more than one whole. An extension for this card sort activity, and one used by Mrs. Orozco, is to ask students to order the cards from least to greatest value. As students work, listen to their rationale for their sorted sets, and press them for their reasoning. See More4U for two video clips of students in Mrs. Orozco's class sharing how they sorted the cards. The vignette shows how Mrs. Orozco provides in-the-moment feedback that supports students' further learning.

0.05	0.099
2.804	0.58
0.025	0.1
0.25	2.84
3.4	0.9

Fig. 4.3. Decimal card sort

TECHNOLOGY INTEGRATION

How can we observe students' thinking in a class of thirty? If you have digital devices in the classroom, students can use a digital platform (such as Educreations, VoiceThread, or Explain Everything) to post a photo of their work and record their thinking. Have students explain how they arrived at their solution—and the reasoning behind their decision making. Many of these online platforms securely store videos on their servers, and some, such as Edmodo, offer options for a parent or guardian to log in with a password to see the student's work. In Chapter 5, you will have an opportunity to see how screencasting tools can be used to create products that can be shared with families. Go to More4U to view a kindergarten student using Educreation to explain his reasoning.

Another idea for card sorts is to give students cards that have various values represented in a variety of ways (e.g., numerical representation, visual representation, and verbal representation), and ask them to sort the cards into categories they can justify. For example, one group working with card sorts on decimal concepts might categorize by the type of representation, while others may categorize by equivalent values across multiple representations (e.g., the number 0.4, a ruler showing 0.4 units shaded, and the words "four-tenths"). You can also make cards that support students' work with arithmetic operations. For example, have students sort several addition problems into sums less than one-half and sums more than one-half. Encourage students to use estimation. Estimating a reasonable answer helps students know whether their answer makes sense. The learning takes place during conversations about how to sort the cards and where to place each card during students' initial group time, as well as during the whole class share-outs that follow (whether in class or online). While students are engaged in the card sort, circulate to listen to their reasoning, and stimulate further thinking by posing questions that may challenge their claims (e.g., "You've said 0.4 is less than one-half. What about 0.40?").

Correct and incorrect

Mathematics education researchers Durkin and Rittle-Johnson (2012, 2015) have found value in asking students to examine and explain pairs of correct and incorrect claims (their research focused on students' knowledge of decimal fractions). The correct and incorrect claims should intentionally illustrate common alternative conceptions, and specific prompts should be given to compare both claims. For example, "Place the value 0.15 on a number line from 0 to 1 divided into 10 equal pieces." Show an example of one correct response and one incorrect response. Then ask students to explain how the two responses are different, why one is incorrect, and what is another way to explain where to place 0.15 (see fig. 4.4; for the full document, see More4U).

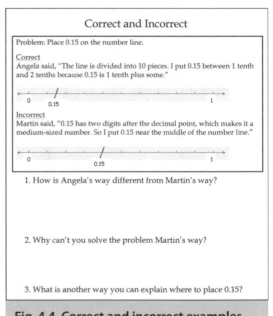

Correct and Incorrect

Problem: Place 0.15 on the number line.

Correct
Angela said, "The line is divided into 10 pieces. I put 0.15 between 1 tenth and 2 tenths because 0.15 is 1 tenth plus some."

0   0.15   1

Incorrect
Martin said, "0.15 has two digits after the decimal point, which makes it a medium-sized number. So I put 0.15 near the middle of the number line."

0   0.15   1

1. How is Angela's way different from Martin's way?

2. Why can't you solve the problem Martin's way?

3. What is another way you can explain where to place 0.15?

Fig. 4.4. Correct and incorrect examples

Remember that assessment is a process: once students generate their responses, it is essential that they receive feedback from peers and from their teacher. Depending on time constraints, you can allow for peer feedback by having students conference with a partner before you collect their work. Once the work is collected, look over each student's paper for evidence of his or her understanding. Provide brief written comments to each student that support further learning. For those whose responses demonstrate strong understanding of the concepts being assessed, pose "what if" questions that stretch their thinking (e.g., "What if the number line went from 0 to 0.5? Where would you place 0.15?"). And for those who are not there yet, provide specific prompts based on their work that guides their thinking about the concept or concepts being developed.

True or false, and why?

With this assessment, students are given a set of claims to evaluate as true or false with justification. This may also be referred to as "agree or disagree, and why?" The claims are created with common alternative conceptions in mind so that the discussions of "why" will allow students opportunities to examine and revise alternative conceptions. For primary grade students, true or false, and why (TFW) claims can ask for a comparison of two expressions; for example, "Is $7 + 5$ the same as $6 + 6$?" or "Is 12×5 the same as 11×6?" In forming their response, students should be encouraged to use figures and manipulatives as well as words. This gives students experience with explanation and justification and represents early informal forms of proof in mathematics.

Figure 4.5 gives an example of TFW claims focused on decimal understanding (see More4U for the full document). Let's look at a claim: "More digits to the right of the decimal point means a smaller value. So 0.0003 is smaller than 0.03 because there are four digits to the

> **True or False...and Why?**
>
> For each CLAIM, decide on your own whether it is TRUE or FALSE...and WHY before discussing with a partner. After discussing with a partner, for each claim, write out the reasons why you believe it is true or false. Be sure to check the claim with more than one example!
>
> CLAIM #1 More digits to the right of the decimal point means a smaller value. So 0.0003 is smaller than 0.03 because there are four digits to the right of the decimal point compared to just two digits.
>
> CLAIM #2 When comparing decimals, just ignore the decimal point and look at the digits. For example, 0.75 is greater than 0.3 because 75 is greater than 3.
>
> CLAIM #3 For decimals, "adding zeros" to the right of a number does not change its value. For example, 0.7 is equivalent to 0.70.

Fig. 4.5. An example of true or false, and why?

right of the decimal point compared to just two digits." On the surface, this seems to be true because 0.0003 *is* less than 0.03. However, the reasoning behind it is not true; more digits in a decimal does not always mean a smaller value because the value of any number depends on the digits in each place value. Students might explain that $^3/_{10000}$ is less than $^3/_{100}$ because $^1/_{10000}$ is less than $^1/_{100}$. They might also offer a counter-example, such as 0.879 is not less than 0.5, and explain how to use their understanding of place value to justify this (e.g., $^{879}/_{1000}$ is greater than $^5/_{10}$ because . . .). Having students justify their claim of true or false will reveal thinking about the important issue of place value in work with decimals.

TECHNOLOGY INTEGRATION

Using multiple formats for students to share their ideas will increase engagement. You might post claims on the class website or use apps such as Socrative, Go Formative, or Kahoot! to invite student responses via digital devices. These digital student response systems (many are free) allow teachers to create quizzes and surveys in which students can reply to prompts and questions in multiple-choice, true/false, or short-answer formats. Many of the response systems include the ability to embed pictures and videos into the questions and allow the teacher to track student progress.

Some good resources to address common alternative conceptions, which are a natural part of the learning process, include NCTM's journals, *Teaching Children Mathematics* and *Mathematics Teaching in the Middle School*, and books such as Richard Ashlock's *Error Patterns in Computation*. The crowd-sourced website Diagnostic Questions (https://www .diagnosticquestions.com) also has many items for mathematics, from basic number and operations through algebra, that may work well for TFW prompts; use the "Questions" tab to freely search by subject and topic (note that it is based in Britain so there are some differences in language about standards).

Assessment of Procedural Knowledge

Procedural knowledge is more than knowing strategies and procedures. NCTM defines procedural fluency (which we refer to as "procedural knowledge") as "the ability to apply procedures accurately, efficiently, and flexibly; to transfer procedures to different problems and contexts; to build or modify procedures from other procedures; and to recognize when one strategy or procedure is more appropriate to apply than another" (2014b).

When you are assessing students' proficiency with procedural knowledge, be sure to examine not only the correctness of the answer but also whether the method used makes sense and is reasonable. Before the advent of computers, speed with hand computation was rightly valued. But since the 1950s, this has become less and less critical, and today's devices that fit in our pockets can out-calculate an entire room full of people (see the Point of Reflection box for more on this). Recent standards for mathematics require students to have deep and flexible knowledge of a variety of procedures, including making choices about which procedures or strategies are appropriate for use for a specific problem, analyzing the results of computations, and connecting mathematical operations to real-world contexts.

For these reasons, there are three primary characteristics of assessments of procedural knowledge:

1. Get at the "how."
2. Examine flexibility in the choice of method (on the basis of what's given and what's known).
3. Ask students to consider the reasonableness of the outcome. (This is the connection to conceptual knowledge.)

"Get at the 'how'" refers to whether students understand the concepts behind the calculations. This requires them to understand and give a rationale for *how* they solve problems because mathematics should always be about sense making and reasoning. Flexibility refers to students' ability to choose a method on the basis of the context of the problem given (for example, if the problem is 7×13, students might notice that it is efficient to mentally find the sum of the products 7×10 and 7×3 to get 91 rather than writing the numbers vertically and using an algorithm). Reasonableness is important so that student calculations are not lost amid mindless symbolic manipulations (e.g., using a learned algorithm) but continually checked against the context of the problem and the properties of numbers.

Compare two methods

Give students a procedural problem, and ask them to use two methods to solve it and then explain which method is best for the given problem. This will provide insight into both the students' flexibility with a given procedure and their ability to interpret the procedure in relation to the given problem. For example, you might ask students to find 15 percent of 60. One method is to write 15 percent as a decimal (0.15) and then multiply by 60.

Another method is to find 10 percent of 60 and add half of that (5 percent) to the outcome to get $6 + 3 = 9$. Use the work generated by students to engage them in a discussion about which method is best for them. This will get them thinking about efficiency and being flexible with procedural knowledge.

Reflecting on strategies and demonstrating procedural proficiency

Students' proficiency with mathematical procedures is strengthened by having them generate multiple solution methods. Students should be expected to provide reasoning and justification for why they use a particular strategy and why that strategy works. It can be challenging for a teacher to monitor the work of every student at the same time when they are asked to demonstrate their proficiency with a specific

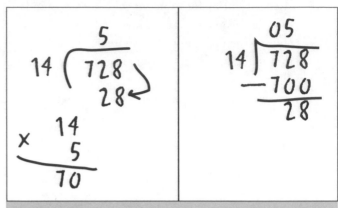

Fig. 4.6. Close-up view of Mrs. Orozco's tablet, showing students' work using the Go Formative app

procedure. Some teachers make use of individual whiteboards that students can hold up to share, while others use technology tools to allow students to share their work (see the Technology Integration textbox for one example).

TECHNOLOGY INTEGRATION

Mrs. Orozco uses the Go Formative app in her classroom. Students work on individual tablets or computers where they find a prompt to work on and space to show their work. On her tablet, Mrs. Orozco can see each student's screen small-scale in real time with their work. This allows her to see the range of strategies used for a given procedure and to identify students who need additional support, as well as students who demonstrate mastery.

The screenshot in figure 4.6 shows a close-up of two students' screens (as seen on Mrs. Orozco's tablet) as they are working on a whole number division problem. It can be productive to have two differing student strategies shared in class or online as part of a teacher-facilitated, student-led discussion of the reasoning behind each one. Finally, think about ways to capture students' ideas so they can be archived and available for later reference. This might be digital but could also take the form of posters for the classroom math wall (see Chapter 1 for more about math walls).

Computer-based assessments of procedural knowledge

When evaluating the merit of a computer-based assessment, keep in mind the three characteristics of assessments of procedural knowledge: get at the how, examine flexibility in the method choice, and ask students to consider the reasonableness of the outcome. Simply having students repetitively input answers to rote arithmetic questions offers little insight into fluency with procedures. A good rule of thumb is to ask, "What information will this assessment generate that informs further teaching and learning?"

Assessment of Factual and Notational Knowledge

Students must become familiar with mathematical facts and notation to support and further their mathematical reasoning. For this reason, demonstrating recall of facts and notation is necessary but not sufficient; for example, students who can write three-fourths as $3/4$ may not actually understand the meaning of fraction notation. In particular, because mathematics as a discipline has been created by humans as a way to represent and then explore abstract ideas, the notation of the subject is important for students to learn and use with precision. This includes the use of symbols, terms, and representations. Assessments that allow students to demonstrate both *knowledge* and *use* of facts and notation will often overlap with assessments of students' conceptual or procedural knowledge. See the Point of Reflection box for insights about the importance of basic facts and how these can be productively learned and assessed.

Here are three characteristics of assessments of factual and notational knowledge:

1. Ask for thinking related to retrieval of facts (e.g., ask, "How did you figure it out?" for students whose responses are not yet at automaticity or for students who cannot name the fact in less time than it takes to use an algorithm to figure it out).

2. Get at precise use of notation (symbols, representations).

3. Promote connections between and among facts, notation, and concepts (e.g., "How can you use your knowledge of 4×7 to figure out 4×14?").

These assessment characteristics ensure that factual and notational knowledge is developed coherently with connections to other types of mathematical knowledge. The examples of assessments we share below illustrate these characteristics.

For decades, timed tests of arithmetic facts and skills have been used to evaluate and rank students by speed and correctness. This communicates the (mistaken) message that mathematics ability is fixed—and speed and correctness are equated with mathematical ability. From the perspective of using assessment to inform teaching and further learning, these practices are simply not that productive. But what about basic facts? Even the Common Core Standards include sets of number facts with which students should develop fluency.

In arguing against timed fact tests, Boaler, Williams, and Confer (2015) claim that fluency is more about number sense than speed. Knowing only that $7 \times 8 = 56$ is less useful than knowing the relationship between 7×8 and 7×7. It is more powerful to know that $7 \times 7 = 49$ and that adding 7 to 49 is equivalent to 7×8. Think about how you support fluency with number sense. For ideas to build fact fluency, see—

- Dr. Valerie Henry's blog (http://ellipsismath.blogspot.com/p/factswise.html);

- Bay-Williams and Kling's article, "Enriching Addition and Subtraction Fact Mastery through Games" (http://www.nctm.org/Publications/teaching-children -mathematics/2014/Vol21/Issue4/Enriching-Addition-and-Subtraction-Fact -Mastery-through-Games/); and

- Kling and Bay-Williams's article, "Assessing Basic Facts Fluency" (http://www.nctm .org/Publications/teaching-children-mathematics/2014/Vol20/Issue8/Assessing -Basic-Facts-Fluency/).

Creating examples and non-examples

To encourage students to be precise in their use of specific facts or notation, challenge them to create examples and non-examples that are closely related. For instance, you might ask students to give you examples and non-examples of expressions that represent a product of 56. This allows them to show multiple ways to create a product of 56, while demonstrating other expressions that are closely related but not equivalent (e.g., values that sum to 56 or factors that make 54 are good non-examples of a product of 56). This helps sharpen or refine students' understanding by calling attention to precision in their use of facts and notation. For this to have the greatest impact, you must require that non-examples be close to being examples, rather than being obvious *non*-examples—a point to keep in mind as you provide feedback on students' responses.

Teacher-student diagnostic interviews

Teacher-student diagnostic interviews, suggested by Kling and Bay-Williams (2014), offer a quick one-on-one way to assess whether students know "just facts and symbols" or have coherent, connected knowledge. The student interviews should be kept short and focused on a specific set of facts or notation. Reflect on how the questions below examine students' thinking and promote number sense (adapted from Kling and Bay-Williams):

- What is 5 + 7?
- How do you know that?
- Can you find 5 + 7 another way?
- If your friend is having trouble remembering this fact, what strategy might help him or her?

Getting at notational knowledge, you could use prompts such as these:

- Write 3 × 5. What does 3 × 5 mean?
- How is 3 × 5 different from 3 + 5?
- How is 3 × 5 related to 4 × 5?

In each case, it is important to capture the data generated from students' responses. Figure 4.7 shows two examples of tables that teachers can use to record information from student interviews. Think about how this sort of information can inform your instructional planning.

(a) Use an accuracy table to review students' progression with addition facts.

Name/facts	Within 5	0, 1, 2	Combinations that make 10	Doubles	Within 10	Within 20
			Foundational facts			
Nicholas						
Kayla						
Cynthia						
Robbie						
⋮						

(b) A table can show the frequency of addition fact strategy use at a glance.

Name/strategies	1 more/ 2 more	Combinations that make 10	Making 10	Doubles	Find 5s	Applies commutativity
Nicholas	+			+	+	+
Kayla	+			+	+	
Cynthia		+		+		+
Robbie	+	+	+			+
⋮						

Fig. 4.7. Tables to record information, generated from student interviews (Kling and Bay-Williams 2014, p. 492)

Assessment of Mathematical Practices

The Standards for Mathematical Practice (also referred to as mathematical practices [MPs]; see fig. 4.8), as delineated in the *Common Core State Standards for Mathematics* (NGA Center and CCSSO 2010), are based on previous research and reasoning from NCTM (NCTM 2000) and the National Research Council (NRC 2001). The mathematical practices have a dual nature. On the one hand, they describe the mathematical ways of thinking, reasoning, and communicating that students should develop while learning mathematics content. On the other hand, they also suggest the type of mathematical activities students will need to engage in to learn mathematics content. These student practices are not skills that can be acquired through direct instruction but rather are habits that emerge and are refined over time as students engage in juicy mathematical tasks, collaborative investigations in mathematics, and thoughtful mathematical discourse. The Inside Mathematics website offers detailed explanations and video examples of students engaged in each of the eight mathematical practices: http://www.insidemathematics.org/common-core-resources/mathematical-practice-standards. If your state or province does not use the *Common Core State Standards for Mathematics*, substitute the mathematical practices or processes that are in your standards document.

1. Make sense of problems and persevere in solving them.

2. Reason abstractly and quantitatively.

3. Construct viable arguments and critique the reasoning of others.

4. Model with mathematics

5. Use appropriate tolls strategically.

6. Attend to precision.

7. Look for and make use of structure.

8. Look for and express regularity in repeated reasoning.

Fig. 4.8. Standards for Mathematical Practice (NCTM 2014a, p. 8)

Here are three characteristics of assessments of mathematical practices:

1. Focus on students' actions and habits as they engage with mathematics tasks.
2. Provide opportunities to examine use of specific mathematical practices.
3. Locate students along a developmental continuum (not "have it" or "don't have it" but to what degree they have it).

Beyond just modeling the mathematical practices for students (which is a good starting point), you need to give students repeated opportunities to engage in these processes themselves and to identify each practice in their own work and in the work of others. Although each mathematical practice has a unique focus, when engaged in mathematical thinking and problem solving, students are often using several of these at the same time because the eight mathematical practices are interconnected and complement one another. Among the assessment ideas below, we have included examples of questions to ask and indicators to take note of as you monitor students' growing proficiency with each of the MPs.

Developing student understanding of the mathematical practices

For younger learners, the language of the mathematical practices is not accessible. One way to introduce the standards and their meaning is to engage students in a juicy task; have students work collaboratively to solve it; and provide opportunity for them to explain, justify, and critique their thinking and the thinking of others. Afterward, connect their actions (e.g., asking themselves whether their strategy makes sense, constructing an argument to defend their thinking) to the mathematical practice. You can even ask students to think about how they would explain what the standard means or what it would look like if they were asked to explain it to someone else (perhaps a family member). Students can create their own posters of what each standard means and looks like in use (figs. 4.9–4.10).

Figs. 4.9–4.10. Student posters of mathematical practices

If you search the Internet for "mathematical practices kid-friendly," you are likely to find several examples of how to make the language more appropriate. One particularly thorough example of this comes from the Jordan School District in Utah where each mathematical practice is written for different grade-level bands with adapted language and examples: http://elemmath.jordandistrict.org/mathematical-practices-by-standard/.

Just as we plan our lessons to address a particular content standard, we must also intentionally design instructional tasks and implement our lessons with one or two of the mathematical practices in mind. Although the description of the Standards for Mathematical Practice is the same across grades, the way these standards look as students engage with and learn more advanced mathematics will change and should grow in sophistication through time. It is important to consider how to incorporate the Process Standards (NCTM 2000) into tasks appropriate for students at your grade. For example, table 4.2 provides explanations and examples of how MP.1 (Make sense of problems and persevere in solving them) may look across three grade bands. What is similar and different in how students engage in MP.1 in these three grades?

Table 4.2. Mathematical Practice 1—Explanations and examples in Grades 1, 3, and 5

MP.1: Make sense of problems and persevere in solving them.	
Grade	**Explanation and example**
1	Mathematically proficient students know that doing mathematics involves solving problems and discussing how they solved them. Students can use concrete tools, pictures, or drawings to explain, conceptualize, and solve such problems as the following: *Mary has some pencils in her school bag. Her mom bought her two more pencils. Now she has seven pencils. How many did Mary start with?* Students may check their thinking by asking, "Does this make sense?" and be willing to try other approaches.
3	Mathematically proficient students know that doing mathematics involves solving problems and discussing how they solved them. Students begin a problem by explaining to themselves what it means, what it is asking for, what methods might be used to solve it, and what sort of tools, pictures, or drawings might be helpful. Students solve problems such as the following: *Carlos bought five boxes of crayons. Each box contains 10 crayons. How many crayons did Carlos buy?* Students monitor their progress by asking themselves, "Does my solution make sense?" Students listen to the strategies of others and make connections between different approaches.

Continued on page 87

Table 4.2. (continued)

5	Mathematically proficient students solve problems by applying their understanding of operations with whole numbers, decimals, and fractions. Students examine the meaning of a problem and look for efficient ways to represent and solve it. Students monitor and evaluate their thinking and change course if needed by asking themselves questions such as "Does this make sense?" "Is this the most efficient way to solve this problem?" "Can I solve it a different way?" Students are able to use more than one method to solve problems such as the following:
	Carlos is making a cake for his sister's birthday and needs 1¼ cups of butter. He looks in the refrigerator and finds ⅔ cup of butter and ¾ cup of butter. Will he have enough butter for the cake? And if so, how much butter will be left over? Explain your reasoning.

Source: Adapted from California Department of Education (2015)

What follows are three examples of assessment tools that not only gauge and promote students' progress toward proficiency with the mathematical practices but also support teachers in planning, analyzing, and reflecting on instruction that supports the MPs.

Teacher questions/prompts

The mathematical practice standards describe the nature of the learning experiences, thinking processes, habits of mind, and dispositions that students need in order to develop deep, flexible understanding of mathematics. One important way to assess students' proficiency with each standard and to examine aligning instruction and task implementation with the MPs is to consider the questions or prompts asked.

Tables 4.3 and 4.4 consist of productive questions or prompts that scaffold students' growth, along with examples of indicators of students' engagement with the specific practice. These can be used informally at the start of the school year, but as students (and teacher) become more familiar with these, we suggest using a data chart (see the Mathematical Practices Recording Chart, downloadable at More4U) to record information about whole-class, small-group, or individual use of the mathematical practices. Depending on your objectives, you might simply tally how often each practice is observed during a targeted time period, or you might make the cells larger and record specific examples of student engagement in one or more practices. You might not want to do this every day, but we recommend setting a schedule for doing this at least once a week so you get a sense of how your students' use of and proficiency with the MPs change over time. For instance, if you notice that early in the school year certain practices are not being used, you might develop a series of lessons that include focus on those practices.

Table 4.3. Prompts and indicators for Mathematical Practice 1: Make sense of problems and persevere in solving them

Questions/prompts to support student use of the practice	Indicators to look for when students are using the practice
Describe this problem in your own words. • What is being asked? • What are you trying to figure out? • What do you already know? • What do you want to know? • How might you draw a picture of this? · • What does this remind you of that you've already learned or used before?	The student talks about what is given and what needs to be figured out and— • explains a process to approach the problem before jumping in right away; • creates representations of the problem; • makes connections to previously learned strategies and content knowledge; • talks about the connections between approaches shared.
How is _____ related to _____?	The student gives examples about similar or related problems.
Why does it make sense to _____?	The student makes frequent reference from work being generated back to the problem context; considers whether his or her strategy makes sense and makes changes if needed.
What is another way you might figure out this problem? How are these two strategies related?	The student uses multiple strategies and makes an effort to understand how the strategies are connected or related.
What did you learn from the incorrect solution you found?	The student demonstrates a willingness to see errors as part of the learning process that provide valuable clues about the qualities of correct approaches.

Table 4.4. Prompts and indicators for Mathematical Practice 2: Reason abstractly and quantitatively

Questions/prompts to support student use of the practice	Indicators to look for when students are using the practice
What are multiple ways you can represent the problem? • With words? • With a drawing or model? • With a mathematical expression?	The student shows multiple representations of the problem that are coherent with one another.
How is this _____ [point to specific value or symbolic expression] related to _____ [point to a specific representation]?	The student translates from decontextualized mathematical symbols to contextualized representations.
What does your result actually mean?	The student provides justification for result, using both mathematical and contextual validity.

Making use of these teacher prompts/questions and student indicators should increase in the level of sophistication with students' experience and development. We have provided examples of these for two mathematical practices and encourage teachers to work collectively with colleagues within a site, system, or digital network to create productive questions and prompts for each of the other six MPs.

Caught in the act

When students are working on a mathematical task, it is fun to challenge them to catch one another in the act of using the MPs. You might decide to focus on one or two specific practices or leave it open to any of them. When a student is "caught in the act" by a peer, she or he receives a "citation" that describes what was observed or heard (see Fig. 4.11 and More4U for a downloadable copy). If students

Caught in the Act Citation

This recording sheet is meant to be used to issue a citation to a student who has demonstrated productive use of one or more of the mathematical practices. Teachers and students alike can be encouraged to pay attention for particularly praiseworthy practices.

You Were Caught in the Act!

Who is being cited? _____

Cited by? _____

You were caught... *(check one or more)*

MP 1	Making sense of problems and persevering in solving them.
MP 2	Reasoning abstractly and quantitatively.
MP 3	Constructing viable arguments and critiquing the reasoning of others.
MP 4	Modeling with mathematics.
MP 5	Using appropriate tools strategically.
MP 6	Attending to precision.
MP 7	Looking for and making use of structure.
MP 8	Looking for and expressing regularity in repeated reasoning.

Evidence *(What was seen and/or heard?)*

Fig. 4.11. Caught in the act citation

have access to digital tools, you can have them snap a photo or record a short audio message about the evidence of what they saw and then share that with a peer.

Math portfolio

The MP self-reflection tool shown in figure 4.12 (full text at More4U) can be part of students' math portfolios in which they have a section for each of the MPs and they select pieces of work that demonstrate their engagement and growth in each. Think about how often you will have students record their reflections and what sort of support you will need to provide. For younger students, offer appropriate language for them to understand what each MP means. Think, too, about the sort of feedback students receive for their portfolio entries. Sticky notes with questions that push on their thinking (e.g., "What is another strategy you might use to get 'unstuck' on a problem?") or comments recognizing growth (e.g., "You did well to explain the connections between the base-ten block model and the number sentence") can be written by teachers and peers alike and then placed in a student's portfolio.

Self-Reflection on My Learning about the Mathematical Practices (MPs)

Mathematical practice Sentence Starter	I have seen this in class when…	I have tried this myself when…	I want to know more about…
MP 1 Make sense of problems and persevere in solving them.			

Fig. 4.12. Mathematical practice self-reflection tool

Thoughts about Large-Scale Summative Mandated Assessments

In most U.S. states and Canadian provinces, there is some form of mandatory end-of-year mathematics assessment for students in specific grades. The primary focus of this chapter is on classroom-based formative assessments; however, it is useful to understand how large-scale standardized assessments may also inform teaching and learning. Teachers need to ask two questions about year-end exams:

1. How can the assessment results be used to inform students' mathematics learning?

Teachers need to know whether (and how) these exams measure students' knowledge of procedures, concepts, and mathematical practices or habits of mind that are part of the standards. Recently developed summative assessments, such as those produced by the Smarter Balanced Assessment Consortium, feature varied item types that attempt to assess deeper knowledge and use computer-adaptive methods that adjust item difficulty (i.e., each student receives a unique set of assessment items on the basis of previous responses) to better match student knowledge of the trait or traits being assessed. Some assessments also use open-response items to get at students' ability to integrate knowledge and skills and communicate mathematical thinking.

What can you infer about students' knowledge of mathematics from students' scores? And how can assessment results (including those from the previous academic year), individual and aggregated, inform learning and instructing? It's just as important to be aware of how scores *cannot* be reliably used. Most large-scale summative assessments are neither designed nor validated to serve as a single, all-encompassing indicator of students' mathematical knowledge; rather, they are meant to be one indicator among several (e.g., grades, portfolios) that together can more fairly and reliably inform instructional and high-stakes decisions (Darling-Hammond, Haertel, and Pellegrino 2015).

2. What strategies and resources are available to monitor students' growth during the school year in areas assessed at the end of the year?

Ideally, scores from end-of-year standardized assessments are not a static snapshot of one-time performance but instead indicate where students fall along a continuum of proficiency or ability and promote continued growth over time. Sixth-grade teacher Jenny Kim Bae has students use information from summative assessments together with other indicators of their mathematical knowledge to write "My Math Learning Goals for the Year" (see fig. 4.13 and More4U for a downloadable

My Math Learning Goals for the Year

Use this as a guide to assist you in setting specific learning goals and help you understand what will be required to meet your goals.

Long-Term Goal (by end of school year)

I will..._____

_____

_____

Short-Term Goal(s)

By the end of _____ trimester, I will..._____

_____

_____

_____

To meet my short-term goal(s), the first thing I need to do is:

I will also need to...

Roadblocks to meeting my goals may be:

Fig. 4.13. Math learning goals form

copy). Having students take time to analyze their formative and summative assessment results to set learning goals gives them a stronger sense of ownership and responsibility for further growth in mathematics. In addition to the summative assessments themselves, there may be interim assessments that can be used during the school year to monitor students' growth in specific sets of standards. If so, make sure that the timing of these is aligned with your instructional calendar, and, as with all assessments, consider how data from interim assessments can serve as a basis for conversations among colleagues and with students about the nature of students' work and the changes or next steps in teaching to best support student learning.

Summary and Reflection

This chapter has focused on ways that teachers can design assessments that address different types of knowledge and that support the deep, meaningful learning of mathematics discussed throughout this book and reflected in standards documents. The use of assessment should both inform instructional decisions and foster students' further learning. Involving students in peer and self-assessment helps them take more responsibility and ownership of their learning. The strategies below summarize some of the key takeaways about the productive use of assessment.

STRATEGIES FOR YOUR CLASSROOM

Considerations for Designing an Assessment-Rich Environment

Articulating clear learning goals

- Understand the larger learning progression within which your current unit fits.

- Identify conceptual, procedural, factual/notational, and mathematical practices knowledge learning goals for each unit.

General considerations for the use of assessment

- Use assessments that elicit students' knowledge and skills in varied formats (individual, pairs, whole class; oral, written, digital).

- Involve students as partners in the assessment (self-assessment and peer assessment).

- Give feedback that is specific and guides further learning for each student.

Assessing conceptual knowledge

- Focus on "why" questions to examine students' reasoning and sense making.

Assessing procedural knowledge

- Focus on "how" questions and students' flexibility with procedures.

Assessing factual/notational knowledge

- Focus on connections among fact, notation, and concepts as well as precise use of notation.

Assessing mathematical practices knowledge

- Focus on students' actions and habits through the lens of specific mathematical practices as they engage with mathematics tasks.

STOP AND REFLECT

Pair with a colleague, and reflect on your use of assessment to inform instruction and further students' learning:

- How does articulating clear goals help make your use of assessment more intentional?

- What strategies have you found effective for eliciting students' conceptual knowledge?

- How do you assess students' flexibility with procedural knowledge?

- What tools do you use to organize information about students' use of mathematical practices?

Chapter 5

Extending the Classroom: Families and Communities

Mathematics is a human activity, a social phenomenon, a set of methods used to help illuminate the world, and it is part of our culture.

—Jo Boaler, *What's Math Got to Do with It?*

A child's first teacher is his or her family, and by "family" we mean *all* the caregivers involved in the child's education—parents, guardians, and other relatives who have a responsibility for his or her care. These caregivers have a tremendous amount of information about their child's activities, interests, and the ways in which he or she excels in school and outside of school. They look ahead and anticipate the opportunities their child will have as she or he continues to learn and grow. Therefore, it makes sense that strong family-school partnerships have been found to contribute significantly to mathematics learning outcomes (Barnard 2004; Jeynes 2005; Patrikakou 2008).

Students come to school with a rich knowledge base about mathematical ideas as a result of their daily experiences within their homes and communities. They develop early number sense and informally learn mathematical concepts through everyday activities: sorting (putting toys or groceries away), reasoning (comparing and building with blocks or deciding which bag of apples to buy to maximize value), representing (drawing to record ideas), recognizing patterns (talking about daily routines and reading predictable books), and using spatial visualization (working with puzzles and digital games) (Clements and Sarama 2000; Janes and Strong 2014; National Council of Teachers of Mathematics [NCTM] 2000). When teachers and schools know and understand students' out-of-school experiences with mathematical ideas, these can be used as a springboard to engage students in formal mathematical thinking and learning (Civil and Andrade 2002; Foote 2011; Moses and Cobb 2001). Mathematics thus becomes not just a subject in school but a way of thinking and reasoning that applies to contexts well beyond the walls of the classroom.

When mathematics learning environments incorporate students' repertoires of practice, "the varied ways people participate in their community's activities" (Gutiérrez and Rogoff 2003, p. 21), students not only see themselves as mathematics learners but see that the curriculum reflects and honors who they are. Students who engage in mathematics learning using their home language, using algorithms from their home culture, and answering questions that are important to them and relevant to needs or interests of their community will see mathematics as a tool to understand and create change in the world around them (Aguirre, Mayfield-Ingram, and Martin 2013; Gutstein 2003; Middleton and Jansen 2011). Strong family-school partnerships that promote bidirectional sharing of information about students, their cultures, and their communities increase the possibilities for creating coherent learning environments across school and home that authentically reflect and respect students' identities. This leads to broader, deeper, and longer-lasting implications for students' mathematics achievement.

STOP AND REFLECT

Think about how you might respond if a colleague asked you the question below. What ideas and questions come to mind?

In what ways do your efforts to promote partnerships with families build on students' knowledge and experiences—their sense of identity—and contribute to students' taking ownership of powerful mathematics?

Family Involvement and Engagement: The Difference—and Why It Matters

Schools traditionally promote a unidirectional form of family participation. Parents are invited to attend school-based functions, to help prepare classroom materials (e.g., cutting out shapes for an activity; copying homework packets), or to chaperone field trips. This one-sided relationship represents power dynamics that exist between school and home (Foote 2011; D. Martin 2006) where the teacher or school decides when and how families may become involved. Research indicates that schooling in the United States best maps onto monolingual, middle-class child-rearing practices (Laureau 2000). For many schools, this leaves many families feeling disconnected from their students' learning.

In his 2011 article "Involvement or Engagement?" Larry Ferlazzo compares two approaches for how families are invited to be partners in students' school learning:

> We need to understand the difference between family involvement and family engagement. One of the dictionary definitions of involve is "to enfold or envelope," whereas one of the meanings of engage is "to come together and interlock." Thus, involvement implies doing to; in contrast, engagement implies doing with. A school striving for family involvement often leads with its mouth—identifying projects, needs, and goals and then telling parents how they can contribute. A school striving for parent engagement, on the other hand, tends to lead with its ears—listening to what parents think, dream, and worry about. (2011, p. 10)

Notice that the common examples shared in the prior paragraph reflect a perspective of family involvement, following the teacher's or school's lead about when and how to participate. Although research suggests some narrow impacts on student outcomes from family involvement, teachers and schools that promote partnerships through authentic engagement see much greater benefits for students, including improved motivation, learning, attendance, and performance at home and at school (Henderson and Mapp 2002; Rothstein 2010).

So, what does family engagement look like in action? Family engagement is about building relationships, listening to and learning from families, and allowing for shared decision making about educational activities. You might notice a parallel here with the ways in which we want students to experience mathematics learning—less through teacher-directed telling and more through guided exploration, collaboration, and communication about mathematical thinking—and the shift from passive family involvement to active, bidirectional family engagement. It is the collaborative, reciprocal relationships with families that have the biggest positive impacts on student learning (Ferlazzo and Hammond 2009; Sheldon and Epstein 2005; Van Voorhis 2011).

Before moving into sharing strategies for family engagement, we briefly touch on the issue of weak family-school partnerships in some schools or within specific populations of students. This condition can result from two situations: when teachers and schools, intentionally or not, create barriers by the ways they structure opportunities for engagement (e.g., timing, language needs, resource needs), and when teachers and schools don't know or understand the ways families already do support children's learning and how to create opportunities to co-construct engagement that is bidirectional (Goodall and Montgomery 2014; Poza, Brooks, and Valdés 2014). In order to nurture the sort of family engagement described above, teachers and school leaders must lead by listening to families and making efforts to learn about the communities and cultures of their students as a means to co-construct bridges between families and schools (Aguirre, Mayfield-Ingram, and Martin 2013;

Foote 2011; Goodall and Montgomery 2014). This includes recognizing that family participation occurs in varied forms and at varied times (both at the school site and outside of the school) and is influenced by many factors, including language, parent education level, attitudes of the school staff, cultural influences, socioeconomic status, and a family member's own experiences that can include anxiety about school or with mathematics (Bartel 2010).

In the rest of this chapter, we offer examples of strategies that draw on students' culture and community to inform meaningful mathematics learning that is connected to their sense of identity. We suggest some ideas for promoting family engagement that leverages the respective strengths schools *and* families bring to supporting student learning. We provide examples from the perspective of the teacher and the classroom as well as that of the school and district to illustrate ways to enact authentic parent engagement.

Teachers and Classrooms

"Effective teachers draw on community resources to understand how they can use contexts, culture, conditions, and language to support mathematics teaching and learning" (NCTM 2014a, p. 65). There are many strategies teachers can use to connect students' mathematical learning to their sense of identity (e.g., culture and community) and to nurture productive partnerships with students' families. Because we recognize that time is a precious and limited commodity for teachers and families, we share ideas that research indicates are likely to have the biggest impact on student outcomes. The critical outcome is a more cohesive learning environment at school and home that enables students to see authentic connections between their daily experiences and their learning of mathematics.

Tapping into students' cultural and community knowledge

Teachers who understand and use learners' cultural and community contexts in meaningful ways are better able to support academic success for their students (Aguirre, Mayfield-Ingram, and Martin 2013; Berry and Ellis 2013; Planas and Civil 2013). When instruction is closely linked to students' lived experiences, students' identities are validated, which, in turn, leads to increased engagement and motivation to learn mathematics (Aguirre, Mayfield-Ingram, and Martin 2013; Boaler 1997; Middleton and Jansen 2011).

The Funds of Knowledge for Teaching (FKT) project is grounded in the theory that students' cultural and community knowledge can provide strategic resources for classroom practice (González, Moll, and Amanti 2005). To get to know students' funds of knowledge, teachers must learn about the day-to-day experiences of students and their families and then use this knowledge as the basis for teaching (Moll and González 1997). Below we offer some suggestions to help you learn about students' interests, ways of knowing, and everyday experiences and how to use this knowledge as an instructional resource.

> **TEACHING TIP: NUMBER OF THE DAY**
>
> Teacher Teri Malpass takes daily attendance with a prompt that has her students reflect on the role of numbers in their academic and cultural experiences. This activity allows her to better understand her students' lived experiences so she can draw upon this knowledge in planning her instruction. See More4U for a video clip showing Ms. Malpass taking attendance as students respond to the prompt: "When you think of the number 12, what comes to mind?"

Math autobiographies and family interviews

Start the school year by having students meet in small groups to explore how mathematics is used in their homes and communities. Encourage them to scour newspapers for numbers and try to give sense to their meaning. Have them interview family members about how they use mathematics and write up their discoveries. As a beginning-of-the-year autobiography, have students create a poster and essay titled "My Personal Numbers!" tying in all the numbers that connect to their lives, such as the number of people in their family, their address, phone numbers, and basketball jersey (see fig. 5.1, and visit More4U for the Personal Numbers Assignment and more student samples). Go beyond an exploration of the self to an exploration of mathematics in the community (e.g., the mathematics in building a garden for the local senior center or examining arrays in the grocery store) and mathematics in our world (e.g., evaluating

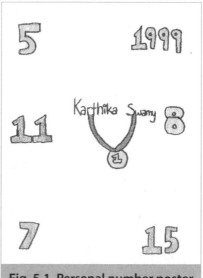

Fig. 5.1. Personal number poster

population growth or water consumption). This activity can serve as the introduction to a yearlong conversation on what we mean by mathematics and why it is important in our lives.

Home visits

Conducting a home visit is a vehicle to better understand students' cultures, values, and traditions; to establish communication and rapport with families; and to consider how to tap into familial resources (e.g., a parent teaches students about quilt making) for more meaningful mathematics learning. Home visits by teachers are occurring in hundreds of schools, and over twenty states have identified this as a core strategy in forging strong family-school partnerships (Ferlazzo and Hammond 2009; Henderson and Mapp 2002; Moll and González 1997). The adapted suggestions that follow were developed by parents and teachers working together in Sacramento, California (see www.teachervisits.org for more).

Preparing for a visit:

- Schedule a home visit at the start of the school year, and offer alternative times. Most visits may need to be in the afternoon or on weekends. (A sample home visit letter is available at More4U.)

- Consider that some families may be familiar and comfortable with home visits, while others may not. Offer alternative places to meet: a local coffee shop, park, or the library.

- Follow up with a brief written note, indicating the exact date and time of the meeting, preferably written in the family's home language.

During the visit:

- Encourage introductions; have everyone explain his or her relationship to the child. Have the student there if possible.

- Find out whether the family has other children in school. What has their experience in school been like? During the home visit, use this conversation starter: "Tell me about your child. What does your child like best about school? What do you want me to focus on this year with [him or her]?"

- Ask the family about their hopes, dreams, and expectations for their student, and share yours.

- Avoid taking notes or recording the conversation during the visit, which can make families nervous. Write down a summary of the visit after you leave.

Continuing interactions with families after the visit:

- Make positive phone calls or send home notes about successes. Be specific with your comments, giving examples of the student's mathematical thinking, perseverance with a tough task, or attention to the thinking and reasoning of others (see More4U for a sample phone call script).

- Provide informal gatherings to discuss mathematics teaching and learning. Have regular opportunities to meet with families for informal conversations to develop a rapport.

- Spend time in the community at places such as the local market, community center, and library.

Applying cultural and community knowledge to inform mathematical tasks

Juicy tasks can be made more powerful by embedding them in a context that has meaning for students (reread the section on "Relevancy" in Chapter 3 for specific strategies related to this). This allows students to share what they already know about the context and connect it to their mathematics learning. It also lends itself to assigning such tasks for homework with instructions for students and families to share how they would each solve the problem. For example, Mayra Orozco asked students to record short interviews with family members about how they use mathematics in their daily lives. One parent, who works as a package handler for a major shipping company, uses mathematics to determine how to most efficiently and safely arrange boxes on the company trucks. Mrs. Orozco used this two-minute clip to spark students' interest in a packaging task in which they explored concepts of volume and surface area (see More4U for the PowerPoint of the task). When students understand what is happening in the context of a problem and have a personal connection to that context, they are more likely to engage and persevere in solving the problem (Boaler 1997; Brenner 1998; Kisker et al. 2012).

Supporting families in understanding new mathematics learning goals

As we have stated previously, recently adopted mathematics standards represent a significant shift in what it means to be proficient in mathematics. When expectations for learning and doing mathematics change, the ways in which families support students must also shift (Shumow 1998). And just as teachers must engage in professional development and collaboration to learn new strategies and perspectives to implement these new standards, similar opportunities must be extended to families. Positioning parents as partners in students' learning while offering opportunities and encouragement to focus on mathematical thinking and reasoning leads to both increased positive family interactions around mathematics and greater academic benefits (Shumow 1998; Van Voorhis 2011). Here are a few suggestions to help you communicate mathematical goals aligned with new standards and ways to prepare families to support student learning at home.

Fostering a Cohesive Vision of Mathematics Learning at School and Home

The mathematics instruction families have experienced in their own schooling is often not the same as the inquiry-focused instruction advocated in current research and adopted mathematics standards (Lehrer and Shumow 1997; Lubienski 2004). Therefore, teachers must find ways to empower parents to understand the mathematics learning occurring in classrooms today and how these methods support success with new learning expectations.

Parents need opportunities to learn what it means to make sense of mathematical ideas, to understand the concepts behind the calculations, to create and refine mathematical justifications, and to develop strategies to support their children by taking on the role of questioner to elicit their children's mathematical thinking (Shumow 1998). These opportunities will strengthen students' learning opportunities and help alleviate potential conflict and dissonance between home and school (Pomerantz, Moorman, and Litwack 2007).

TECHNOLOGY INTEGRATION

Kelley Otani teaches kindergarten and uses a web-based media-sharing site to communicate with families what it means to engage in problem-based mathematics in her classroom. At the start of the year, she video-records whole-group discussions to share the type of mathematical discourse taking place in class and the type of questions she asks to elicit and extend students' thinking (see fig. 5.2, and view a sample of Mrs. Otani's videos at https://www.educreations.com /lesson/view/cgi-using-the-100s-board /34154911/?s=fbKyVW). Mrs. Otani digitally records students solving problems to highlight each student's problem-solving strategy. She then emails the video to each family to share their thinking.

Fig. 5.2. Video recording of classroom math talks

As we share in the final chapter, Mrs. Orozco and her colleagues organize interactive family mathematics nights where they engage entire families (everyone is welcome!) in tasks that mirror the work being done in classrooms and discuss with the adults how these sorts of activities support children's reasoning and sense making in mathematics. The teachers have found these sessions effective in providing parents with authentic hands-on experiences with new expectations of mathematics learning while, at the same time, validating families' prior knowledge of mathematics.

Homework support

The assignments students bring home from school communicate to families what is valued and how teachers expect children and families to interact around mathematics. If teachers frequently send home worksheets of skill practice, they are sending the message that algorithmic practice is what matters. This is likely to encourage parents to check for correctness and to show their children "how I would do it" with little attention to mathematical

USING TECHNOLOGY TO ENGAGE FAMILIES

Technology can strengthen connections and communication between school and home and help overcome barriers of time and transportation that limit engagement. Below are some suggestions:

- **Videoconferencing.** Web-based audio and video calling apps allow teachers to meet remotely with students and families. Many of these apps, such as Google Hangouts and Skype, allow videoconferencing with multiple participants. Some also feature messaging, screen sharing, and the ability to record and archive the conversation for others to view later. These apps can be used for parent-teacher conferences, virtual family nights, and remote tutoring.

- **Classroom websites.** A class website can be used for information sharing (e.g., posting instructional information and activities, directory of links, and student work) and as a bidirectional communication tool. Posting assignments, examples of student work, and links to additional resources gives families greater access to materials that might support their efforts to help their children. Websites can also be used to post surveys about specific topics you would like to learn more about from families to extend your knowledge of students' communities and cultures. In Christine Bouma's fifth-grade class, a student pair is assigned the role of news editor each day. Throughout the day, their job is to take pictures and post summaries of class activities for the classroom webpage.

- **School or district resource sites.** With so many people connected to the Internet, it can be effective to create resource pages for parents that reflect the mathematics learned in school and suggestions to extend learning at home. The Howard County Public School System in Maryland has developed a particularly comprehensive mathematics education site for parents and families: http://hcpssfamilymath.weebly.com/. This site promotes productive engagement between parents and students by offering rich mathematics tasks to try out at home and examples of strategies for adults to foster children's mathematical thinking. The district has partnered with the Howard County Public Library to offer online homework help. This is an excellent example of school-community partnership to support student success.

sense making. Alternatively, teachers communicate a different message—that the process of mathematical thinking is valued—when they send home problems that ask students to explain a process, compare two methods of carrying out an arithmetic operation, solve a problem rooted in a familiar cultural or community context, or interview a family member about his or her thinking about a specific mathematical problem.

In her research, Lee Shumow (2003) found that assignments asking for more than algorithmic practice promoted more productive interactions between students and adults, resulting in less controlling assistance and more elaborative assistance as adults tried to support students' thinking. Table 5.1 describes controlling approaches adults use to help students that reflect a narrow view of mathematics as rules and procedures to follow. Suggestions for alternative approaches reflective of elaborative support are better aligned with new learning expectations.

Table 5.1. Adult helping behaviors: Controlling versus elaborative

Before (controlling)	Now (elaborative)
Check the child's homework for accuracy: focus on correct answers.	Ask the child to explain his or her thinking and reflect on the process of solving. Try to make connections to other problems he or she solved that week.
Explain the steps to the child so he or she can replicate the procedure.	Let the child work through the problem before you intervene. Students should develop conceptual understanding before procedural fluency and memorization. Link the child's explanation to his or her understanding.
Make sure the child does many problems of the same type.	Give children fewer problems, and encourage the use of multiple strategies.
Drill students to memorize facts.	Realize that children's mathematical thinking is developmental. Encourage the child to use related facts and relational thinking to learn new facts and solve problems.

STOP AND REFLECT

Take a moment to consider the mathematics assignments you typically ask students to complete at home.

1. What might be important for families to know about the goals you have for students' mathematics learning?

2. What efforts can you make (or have you made) to help families understand and support their children's mathematics learning?

While we are on the topic of homework, let's consider a few examples of mathematics homework that might be assigned during a third-grade unit on fraction concepts that emphasizes sense making more than rote practice. As you read each prompt, think about what sort of learning goal is being supported and how a parent or other adult might help a child with it. Notes for the teacher are in square brackets.

1. Explain what a fraction is to someone in your household.

2. Explain what $3/4$ looks like to someone in your household.

3. Write down four things around your house that represent $3/4$.

4. Shade in $3/4$ in as many ways possible using the squares on this page. [See More4U for two versions of a page with blank squares.]

5. For each representation, explain why it represents $3/4$. Then choose two of the representations and explain how they show $3/4$ differently. [Examples include set models; part-whole relationships; number line models; and realia, such as $3/4$ of a stick of butter, $6/8$ of a cake, or nine out of twelve items.]

6. For each fraction, explain whether it is smaller than, equal to, or larger than $3/4$ and why. Use symbols and words. [Use no more than four fractions, including at least one that is equivalent to $3/4$.]

In each example, students are asked to reason about fractions in general and $3/4$ in particular. The depth of knowledge increases steadily from simple recognition to multiple representations to argumentation. In this example, at the start of the unit, the teacher's communication with parents might mention the importance for later learning of students' early understanding of the concept of fraction and equivalent fractions. This teacher would want parents to know that students' thinking and reasoning about fractions will expand through a series of intentionally designed learning activities, both in the classroom and outside of it. The teacher might follow up with parents by providing links to web-based resources they can use to explore this further.

School- and District-Level Efforts for Family Engagement

While the efforts of one teacher to engage families are important, family engagement efforts can and should go beyond a single classroom. Indeed, the strongest family-school partnerships involve the entire school community—the school staff and families—united around a common vision for students' growth and development (Weiss et al. 2009). Successful family-school partnerships, while unique to each site and community, have common characteristics: both partners (families and school staff) are viewed as equally valuable contributors; barriers for families' involvement are acknowledged and addressed; and parents are given opportunities to contribute to school decision making and governance (Henderson and Mapp 2002). Following are two examples of strategies for increasing family engagement at the school or district level; they are based on work we've done with teachers, with specific attention to strengthening mathematics learning outcomes.

CONNECTING FAMILIES TO ACADEMIC EFFORTS

Jean Pryor, a sixth-grade mathematics teacher at John Burroughs Middle School, sought to address inequities in her school. Noticing that the magnet program did not reflect the ethnic composition of the student body, she created programs to support students and their families.

Ms. Pryor created academic-focused parent nights. Four nights per year, she invited parents to engage in activities, vocabulary, and sample assessment items that their children would experience in the coming weeks. Equipped with notebooks and pencils, parents worked collaboratively through these lessons to better understand student thinking, possible alternative conceptions, and ways to assist student learning without taking over their thinking.

Over the course of the first year, Ms. Pryor saw 80 percent of the parents in at least one session and many parents for multiple sessions. Her students scored an average of 94 percent on their district periodic assessment data. She reports that she gained more from these parent workshops than the amount of work it took to prepare for them. Connecting families to academic efforts, rigor, and expectations provided a setting for parents, students, and teacher to have meaningful conversations about mathematics learning.

Co-facilitating parent workshops: Building from parent interests

Teachers and site leaders communicate messages to families and communities about what is valued through the sort of activities offered to promote engagement. When such plans are made with a keen awareness of local interests and resources, and in collaboration with parents and other adults who share an interest in furthering student success, a unified vision for family-school engagement can emerge. One such example is from William Green Elementary School in Lawndale, California.

William Green Principal Jenny Padilla and mathematics instructional coach Vanessa Hayward noticed that many parents were participating in school-organized evening activities at the school that were focused on healthy living (including taking Zumba classes!). Recognizing this interest and commitment to healthy living, Ms. Padilla and Ms. Hayward partnered with the district's nutrition services staff and leaders to discuss ideas about how to build on their seminars on healthy living to introduce some of the new approaches to learning mathematics. This collaboration led to the creation of seminars, co-facilitated by teachers, district staff, and local community members, that engaged families in mathematics investigations around food choices, serving sizes, and the Standards for Mathematical Practice. These topics provided an entry point into mathematics practices parents later observed in classrooms during structured learning walks that the principal set up. Recognizing and then building on the interests of the community enabled this team to introduce parents to shifts in teaching and learning mathematics and to mathematical concepts their children were learning, all while generating a strong sense of agency among all involved.

Parent observations in a second-grade math classroom

Parents working collaboratively during the math sessions

STOP AND REFLECT

How has the partnership at William Green Elementary School—

- created a *physical environment* to connect parents' knowledge and experiences to the mathematics students are learning?
- considered *tasks* that engage families in meaningful mathematics?
- created a *discourse environment* across multiple stakeholders (students, teachers, parents, site leadership) to support mathematics learning?
- disrupted traditional power dynamics between school and home by engaging a larger community of mathematics learners?

Connecting teacher professional development efforts with simultaneous parent workshops

District-wide parent engagement initiatives can have multiple benefits, providing opportunities for cross-campus, cross-community collaboration. By combining resources (both human resources as well as financial resources), districts can provide multiple and diverse opportunities for family engagement.

Having multiple teams within one large-scale project distributes the work of creating materials, leaving more time for debriefing and reflection, and can lead to greater sustainability. The example that follows comes from Carolee Hurtado's work with the Manhattan Beach Unified School District (MBUSD). As MBUSD was in the process of transitioning teaching to newly adopted state mathematics standards and teachers were engaged in professional development and coaching opportunities, parents began to notice changes in homework and classroom routines, and they began to question and comment on these. Sensing an opportunity for partnership, the district reached out to parents via electronic and printed surveys to invite their questions and concerns.

The responses informed the district's development of a series of seminars aimed at both supporting teachers' classroom-based efforts and fostering stronger family understanding of and connections to the changes in mathematics curriculum and methodology. These sessions communicated the vision of mathematics learning and the time line for the transition to new standards, engaged parents in mathematical activities that mirrored classroom practices, presented educational research that supported their instructional methodologies, and offered suggestions for promoting mathematical discourse at home. Some sessions were designed for parents and children to engage in mathematics workshops together. The sessions also provided families with a space to bring their voice to the table and to offer suggestions for what they felt would benefit their children and strengthen the mathematics program.

One recent parent workshop focused specifically on helping parents of fourth-grade students understand connections between research and practice around the importance of mathematical discourse, experience what mathematics learning looks like in fourth grade, and recognize what parents can do at home to support children's success in mathematics. The UCLA Mathematics and Parent Projects (led by Carolee Hurtado) partnered with MBUSD district leadership and teacher Holly Compton to lead the workshop. After being asked to solve a division problem ("If three pounds of oranges sell for 87 cents, how much does one pound sell for at the same market?"), parents shared strategies with each other, participated in a whole-group share, and then were invited to analyze student work from the same problem.

Ms. Compton had carefully selected an example of student work (see fig. 5.3) that would highlight multiple strategies and provide evidence of student understanding. The student had illustrated four strategies to solve the problem: an area model of multiplication where the student partitioned 87 into 60 and 27 and found factors that would multiply by 3 to give each of these areas; a graphic organizer showing 87 decomposed into 60 and 27 and then each divided by 3 (thus using the distributive property of multiplication over addition); a depiction of the standard U.S. algorithm for long division credited to a classmate; and two number sentences: with the sum of 29 below these. Some parents were convinced that the work sample could not have been created by a fourth grader. By chance, the mother of the child who created this work was in the room, and the teacher had discreetly let her know. It was a very moving moment when this mother expressed joy, excitement, and surprise as she talked about her child's learning challenges with mathematics and how she had seen such an improvement this year in disposition and academic success. At that point, this parent engagement session moved from parents learning from the teacher and

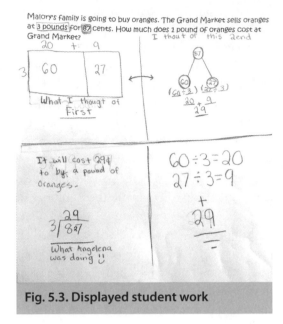

Fig. 5.3. Displayed student work

district to mutual learning and respect, where all participants learned from each other and became even more committed to the work being done to improve students' learning of mathematics.

Summary and Reflection

This chapter focused on the importance of families and communities. Strong family-school partnerships that promote bidirectional sharing of information provide a more cohesive vision of learning across school and home and increase the possibilities for creating learning environments that reflect and respect our students' identities, which, in turn, lead to broader and richer opportunities for mathematics learning. Strategies to promote family engagement can occur at the classroom and school or district level.

STRATEGIES TO PROMOTE FAMILY ENGAGEMENT

Classroom level

- Build rapport with families so they feel comfortable engaging in conversations with teachers and school personnel. Promoting family engagement in the absence of trusting relationships can be difficult.

- Tap into students' cultural and community funds of knowledge through home visits and classroom assignments that encourage students to share and investigate how mathematics is used in their home and community.

- Consider both in-person engagement experiences and experiences via technology. Technology can be used to engage families in understanding new mathematical learning goals through videoconferencing and through classroom, school, and district resource sites.

School and district level

- Plan parent workshops with an awareness of local interests and resources and in collaboration with parents and the local community.

- Provide parent workshops that allow families to engage in the mathematical discourse and experiences with mathematics learning fostered in the classroom.

- Celebrate students' and parents' multiple problem-solving methods, and highlight the understanding within their thinking.

STOP AND REFLECT

Before you move on to the last chapter, pair with a colleague during a grade-level or schoolwide meeting to reflect on these questions:

- How do you elicit and build on students' cultural and community funds of knowledge in your teaching?

- How do you and your school provide bidirectional sharing of information?

- What could you do to provide more opportunity for students and families to have voice in the curricular and instructional decision making at the classroom and school level?

- What comes to mind as a way to move toward a model of parent engagement that focuses on family and school partnerships?

Chapter 6

Moving from Vision to Reality: Bringing the Elements Together

The previous five chapters unpacked each of the five elements of powerful mathematics learning environments: the physical and virtual space, mathematical discourse, tasks, assessments, and families and communities. In this chapter, we illustrate the convergence of these five elements in practice by highlighting some of the ways in which three teachers support all students in taking ownership of mathematical knowledge and developing mathematical habits of mind. We present and discuss each classroom in terms of the three principles discussed throughout the book:

1. Teach toward the understanding of powerful mathematics.
2. View students as sense makers with valuable, important ideas.
3. Nurture a mathematics community of learners.

Classroom 1: Jean Chen-Wu, Kindergarten

Mrs. Jean Chen-Wu teaches kindergarten at A. E. Arnold Elementary School in Cypress, California. Mrs. Chen-Wu's class is made up of twenty-five students. The school is rich in linguistic and cultural diversity with 30 percent Latino, 33 percent Asian American, 25 percent European American, and 5 percent African American. The majority of the students enter school speaking two or more languages.

Mrs. Chen-Wu has taught for eighteen years and has actively participated in and led mathematics professional developments on Cognitively Guided Instruction (CGI). CGI (Carpenter 1985; Carpenter et al. 1989) is a professional development program in which teachers learn about the development of children's mathematical thinking and instructional strategies that use students' thinking to inform instructional decisions.

As a kindergarten teacher, Mrs. Chen-Wu knows that for many of her students their first experience with school mathematics is in her classroom. Therefore, she has developed a classroom environment in which the learning of mathematics is integrated across disciplines and embedded throughout their daily classroom routines.

The role of context is a critical component of her math instruction. Situations from real life serve as a wonderful context for math investigation. In a recent interdisciplinary lesson, the class learned about the Inuit culture as they built their own igloo out of milk jugs (fig. 6.1). Throughout the design and construction process, students had plenty of opportunities to actively engage in early mathematical concepts: counting, geometric and spatial reasoning, patterns, and estimation. Mrs. Chen-Wu also uses the daily classroom routines as opportunities for math exploration. The following episode, which takes place in December, three months after the start of the school year, provides an example.

Mrs. Chen-Wu's students represent a wide range of ability in their understanding of basic mathematical concepts and skills. The majority of students can now solve a variety of word problems by modeling the action in the problems by using counters and other materials, but they are still developing their understanding of place value and base-ten number concepts and the use of more abstract strategies for solving problems. Mrs. Chen-Wu builds on this diversity in a number of ways.

Fig. 6.1. A milk jug igloo

Opening activity

The students are sitting in rows in the whole-class meeting area. They have no paper, pencil, or other math tools in hand. The day begins with the class taking attendance. Observe how Mrs. Chen-Wu makes taking attendance an exploration of place value and number relationships (see More4U for a template of the attendance double ten-frame).

Mrs. Chen-Wu:	Let's see who is here today.

[*The boys in class take turns counting off out loud one at a time: "One, two, three, ..." After the last boy counts off "eleven," Mrs. Chen-Wu calls on Brandon to write the number 11 on the board and to represent 11 on the ten-frame. The students count with Brandon as he places one blue circle at a time to represent 11 on the ten-frame. Then, the class repeats the same activity to find the number of girls in class—the girls counting off out loud one at a time until the last girl counts off "eleven." Joselyn is called up to write the number 11 on the board and to represent 11 with green circles on the ten-frame.*]

Mrs. Chen-Wu:	How many boys and girls are here today? Think to yourself first. Just in your head. Don't share with anyone yet.

[*Mrs. Chen-Wu gives a minute of wait time.*]

Mrs. Chen-Wu:	Now, whisper to your partner how many students are here today and how you figured it out. Listen closely to your partner; I may call on you to explain your partner's thinking.

[*Student pairs turn to face each other and whisper their response.*]

Mrs. Chen-Wu:	Now, sit criss-cross applesauce. So, how many people are here today? Nolan, what did your partner say?
Nolan:	Twenty-two.
Mrs. Chen-Wu:	And how did he get twenty-two?
Nolan:	There's ten blues and ten greens. Then, there's two more.
Mrs. Chen-Wu:	So, you said, there's ten blues and there's ten greens [*Mrs. Chen-Wu touches the ten-frame with the ten blue circles and then the ten-frame with the green circles.*] So, the ten and ten makes . . .
Class:	Twenty.
Mrs. Chen-Wu:	Then, there are two more?
Nolan:	That makes twenty-two.
Mrs. Chen-Wu:	Did anyone's partner solve it differently? Martha?
Martha:	Sammy counted five, ten, fifteen, twenty, twenty-one, twenty-two.
Mrs. Chen-Wu:	Sammy counted by fives.
Taylor:	We're only missing two.

Students in class: We're missing two.

Mrs. Chen-Wu: How did you figure out that we're missing two students? Whisper to your neighbor how you figured it out.

STOP AND REFLECT

How has Mrs. Chen-Wu designed—

- the physical environment to provide space for students to work individually and collectively as mathematical thinkers? How does Mrs. Chen-Wu prepare students for partner share?

- the discourse environment with participation structures, routines, and strategies to engage *all* students in mathematical discourse? Why does Mrs. Chen-Wu have students explain their partner's strategy and not their own?

- the task environment to encourage students' development of conceptual understanding and mathematical habits of mind?

Classroom 2: Señora Jones, Dual Immersion, Third Grade

Mark Twain Elementary School is located in Lawndale, California. The school is diverse with the student population consisting of 63 percent Latino, 12 percent Asian American, 12 percent European American, and 7 percent African American. Over half of the students qualify for free or reduced lunch, and approximately 40 percent of the students are considered English language learners.

Señora Cherise Jones teaches third grade in a dual-language program. The goal of the program is to support students in developing bilingual and biliteracy skills in Spanish and English. Sra. Jones teaches mathematics primarily in Spanish. For the past several years, Sra. Jones has participated in a voluntary, district-funded CGI professional development program and another project with UCLA-Stanford on Early Childhood Education Mathematics to promote instructional practices that nurture a community of learners.

Sra. Jones establishes various classroom structures that promote collaboration in learning mathematics. Students are held accountable for attending to and contributing to one another's ideas. Sra. Jones believes that productive mathematical discourse occurs when students own the language of the discipline. A poster of sentence starters is visible, and students are encouraged to use the sentence starters during their daily number talk. The following episode takes place in January and exemplifies a typical day in her class with students actively engaged in mathematical discourse and mathematical reasoning.

Students are gathered in the classroom meeting area, with no tools or pencils—the focus is on engaging in talk around their reasoning and sense making. Sra. Jones writes the following equation on the board:

$$4 \times (20 + 5) = 4 \times (\square + 10 + 5)$$

The values and operations in the equation were carefully chosen to encourage students to reason about equality through relational thinking. Sra. Jones selected numbers that would scaffold students toward understanding that the equals sign means "the same as" and the two expressions in the equation represent the same value. Students were asked to figure out, without computing, what value would go in the box to make the equation true. This problem builds on months of prior work with properties of addition and multiplication as well as grouping tasks.

After allowing some individual think time, Sra. Jones asks students to share their initial ideas, and she simply records the responses offered without evaluating them: 20, 2, and 10. The following whole-class discussion ensues.

Sra. Jones: Who would like to provide justification for one of these responses?

Sarah: I would like to defend 2. When I look at the equations, I know that what's in the parentheses is going to be multiplied times 4. So if the numbers in the parentheses are the same, then it will be the same. So 2 times 10 is 20 and 5 more is 25. On the other side, it's 20 plus 5 that is also 25.

Sra. Jones: Any responses or reactions?

Camila: I was thinking the same thing as Sarah that the number in the parentheses needs to be the same. On the left, it's 20 plus 5, 25 and on the right I put in the number 10. 10 plus 10 is 20 and 5 is 25.

Sra. Jones: Sarah and Camila explained their thinking in similar ways but Sarah used 2 and Camila used 10.

[*Silence*]

Sra. Jones: Turn to your partner and see if we can determine how it is possible that Sarah and Camila used different numbers to make this equation true.

[*Chatter*]

Sra. Jones: Let's hear what you discussed in your partnerships.

Sarah: I'd like to revise my thinking. My partner helped me to see that it says box plus 10 plus 5. I thought it said box times 10 plus 5.

[*Lots of students are holding up one hand with the thumb and pinky finger extended and the other fingers closed, a signal for "agreement" borrowed from American Sign Language.*]

Bo: Sarah's explanation made perfect sense when she was saying it. I didn't even realize there was a problem until I heard Camila's explanation, but I didn't know what was wrong.

Estrella: If we wrote out the equation like Sarah said it, then it would also be true, right?

Sra. Jones: Discuss that with your partner. If this [*Sra Jones circles the "+" symbol*] was a multiplication symbol, would 2 make the equation true?

Daniel: It would because $10 + 10 + 5$ is the same as 2 groups of 10 plus 5. You can see the two groups of 10.

STUDENTS' COMMENTS ABOUT THEIR LEARNING ENVIRONMENT

Below are responses from two students who were asked to share their thoughts about what it is like to learn mathematics in Sra. Jones's class.

In math, we talk about a lot of topics. Like if it is real or fake [true or false]. We talk about strategies to figure out if [a number sentence] is fake or real. If it works. Like is $10 + 3 + 2$ the same as $3 + 10 + 2$. It helps us to talk about our ideas because they might tell me I was wrong and I say I think I was right. It helps make us smarter. We get smarter when talking about our ideas because it makes us think about it more.

—Daniel, Sra. Jones's third-grade class

What I like about math is that there are lots of strategies you can use. It's not just one plus one is two. It's like you can do so many strategies. Learning math is really fun. It's not boring. It's because there are so many things we learn. It's not that here is a sheet of paper for you to just do. My teacher doesn't just make us do something once and say now you have learned math. It's like we keep working on it. Talking about math or writing it down helps us learn. We do talk to a partner. But we also talk to everyone in the class. We didn't do that in the other grades. Before we just talked to a partner, but this time we get to share our ideas with everyone. That helps because then people can add on to your ideas to make it easier for me to get it. And I say oh yeah, now I get this strategy.

—Lilia, Sra. Jones's third-grade class

Sra. Jones: Let's take a moment to discuss the option of 20.

[*No one volunteers to defend 20.*]

Sra. Jones: What might be a reason that a student could think that 20 makes the equation true?

Jesus:	On the left the first number is a 20 and on the right the first number is box. So maybe someone just thought if you put the 20 on the other side, then it would be true.
Jacquie:	Yeah, I was thinking the same thing. Maybe someone just looked quickly and thought that the missing number was a 20 because they saw a 20 on the other side and it wasn't on this one.
Sra. Jones:	How do we know that 20 does not make the equation true?
Jesus:	It would make the equation true if we didn't have the ten. If it just said parenthesis box plus 5 then it would be 20.
Jacquie:	20 in the box would make it 20 plus 10 plus 5 and that is 35. Then we would have $4 \times 25 = 4 \times 35$ and those are going to be different.

STOP AND REFLECT

How has Sra. Jones—

- designed a task environment that sets students up for productive participation within a discourse-rich environment? Why might Sra. Jones work so diligently to create opportunities for students to revise their thinking?
- simultaneously used student talk to informally assess students' thinking and make instructional decisions based on what she hears and sees?
- established norms for discourse that encourage students to learn from each other?

Classroom 3: Mrs. Orozco (and Colleagues), Dual Immersion, Fifth and Sixth Grade

Mrs. Mayra Orozco teaches at Adelaide Price Elementary School in Anaheim, California, in a fifth-grade dual immersion (English/Spanish) program. About three-fourths of her students qualify for free or reduced lunch, and one-half have a home language other than English (typically Spanish). Working with a faculty member from California State University at Fullerton, Professor Armando Martinez-Cruz, Mrs. Orozco and her colleagues—Marcela Guerrero, Maribel Reyes, Christina Garcia, and Jenny Franke—created a series of four one-hour family engagement sessions for their fifth- and sixth-grade classes. This grew out of their involvement with a grant-funded project (National Science

Foundation award #1321339, Transforming Academic and Cultural Identidad through Biliteracy) to promote stronger cultural and community connections in mathematics and science lessons.

The intent of the family sessions was to model learning mathematics with understanding by engaging families in meaningful mathematical tasks (the type of juicy tasks discussed in Chapter 3) that reflect realistic contexts related to the experiences and community contexts of parents and students. Community and family contexts were gathered during the prior school year when Mrs. Orozco and her colleagues had students video-record a short interview in which they asked a parent or guardian, "How do you use math every day?" These brief clips were used to motivate mathematics learning in the current school year (see two of these at More4U) and were featured in two of the family engagement sessions.

The teachers had two goals in mind for these sessions. First, they wanted parents and students to spend time thinking mathematically about a problem in order to model the sort of reasoning and sense making expected from students and the kind of habits or practices that support this. Second, they wanted parents to experience how mathematical understanding is being developed differently and more deeply than what they may have experienced in their own schooling. This included ideas of building on students' thinking to refine mathematical knowledge, valuing multiple methods to solve one problem, and using discourse as a tool for making sense of mathematics.

Each of the two sessions, one of which is described in detail below, began with watching a short video clip of a parent talking about her use of mathematics in everyday life. This was meant to generate a personal connection to a mathematics problem. Then a task related to the clip was introduced, and groups of people (adults and children) were asked to work on the problem collaboratively. The teachers circulated through the room, just as they would during a school-day lesson, and probed with questions that elicited people's thinking. After some work time, the groups shared specific solution strategies with a focus on the rationale for a given approach and connections from the mathematical work back to the original problem context. Discussion followed about why different approaches were mathematically justified and whether one method might be more efficient than others. Finally, Dr. Martinez-Cruz concluded the workshop with an exploration of a related mathematical topic and discussion about why this sort of learning is important for preparing students for later concepts and courses.

The first session in this series started with a video clip interview of a parent who works as a supervisor at a catering company. She shared her use of mathematics to determine how many tables and chairs are needed for an event, how many staff will be required, and what the cost for the food will be. A problem based on this clip was created about planning for a quinceañera (ceremony for girls turning fifteen) that would require the use of multiplication (which was the mathematical focus of the session). Each family had a handout with the problem and a diagram of the layout of the event room (see More4U for a copy). They were asked to figure out how many people would be able to attend and how much this would cost. Parents and students worked collaboratively on the problem and talked about their approaches. Most of the parents carried out multiplication by using the standard U.S. algorithm (lining up the two values vertically, finding products of pairs of digits, and summing the results).

After solution strategies were shared, Dr. Martinez-Cruz discussed some of the challenges students have with using the traditional multiplication algorithm, including losing track of zeros and misaligning products. He then introduced another method for multiplication, a rectangular area model (which he refers to as the "box method"), that more transparently shows the place value of each digit being multiplied (see More4U for a video of this segment). Parents and children spent time working out three multiplication problems using the rectangular area method. When invited to share their comments, some parents said the area method seemed more complicated, while others noted that it allowed them to see more clearly the values being multiplied at each step. Dr. Martinez-Cruz and Mrs. Orozco closed the session with a discussion of how the area method can extend to multiplication of polynomials in algebra, and they highlighted how the area method helped many students better understand multiplication and place value by making the value of each digit visible (see More4U for a short video clip of the closure).

This sort of session is powerful in that it honors the methods parents are familiar with while, at the same time, it introduces them to methods that might be less familiar. This helps mitigate some of the anxiety parents have about "new" approaches to learning mathematics and the work their children bring home that in some cases is difficult for parents to understand. Through these sessions, parents learn that, in the 21st century, students' mathematical reasoning is valued over rote computation, and they develop the sense that it is okay to learn with their children.

STOP AND REFLECT

How have Mrs. Orozco and her colleagues—

- connected family and community knowledge and experiences to the mathematics students are learning?

- created a bidirectional relationship with parents as partners in supporting children's mathematics learning?

- modeled a task environment that encourages development of conceptual understanding and mathematical habits of mind?

Discussion

The activities in these three classrooms illustrate perfectly the three principles highlighted through this book.

Principle 1: Teach toward the understanding of powerful mathematics.

A central premise of this book is that students' understanding should be the most fundamental goal of mathematics instruction. This understanding is characterized by the development of mathematics knowledge through processes of reasoning and sense making and with coherence so that learning is connected to students' identities and experiences as well as prior mathematical knowledge (Brownell 1935; Hiebert and Carpenter 1992). The nature of the three activities described above and the roles of the teachers, the students, and their families reflect a culture of exploration and collaboration that supports the learning of mathematics with understanding.

This can be seen in Mrs. Chen-Wu's class when she takes attendance by using the double ten-frames, a ten-structured organization, to facilitate students' development of number sense within the context of five and ten. This daily activity develops students' ability to compose and decompose numbers (e.g., seeing 14 as composed of ten and four or six away from twenty or five, five, and four). The ability to look at a number flexibly and relationally (in relation to other numbers) serves as a foundation for students' future work with arithmetic and algebra.

This can be seen in Sra. Jones's class through her opening moves and strategic use of questioning and responding and through how she orients students to each other's thinking throughout the lesson. These intentional teacher moves activate students' prior knowledge and hook student engagement. Through her questioning and revoicing of student thinking, Sra. Jones uses language as a tool to inquire and prompt small- and whole-group discussions around specific mathematical goals.

This can be seen in Mrs. Orozco's class through the intentionality of bringing parents and students together to engage in a mathematical modeling task that encourages and values diverse approaches. The facilitators focused on how parents use mathematics in their lived experiences, gave background on the context, highlighted multiple strategies, and introduced strategies designed to provide conceptual understanding of mathematics. They further developed these ideas by demonstrating how and why building on student thinking is important for conceptual foundations and for later learning.

Principle 2: View students as sense makers whose ideas are valuable and important.

In the past, schools have conditioned students to think of ideas as being right or wrong, correct or incorrect, true or false (Hiebert and Lefevre 1986; Mullis et al. 2012). When the desired outcome is student ownership of rich mathematics knowledge and habits of mathematical reasoning, it is more productive to presume student responses, either right or wrong, are the result of their thinking. Children are all sense makers, and deep learning must build from what makes sense to them.

Mrs. Chen-Wu consistently responds to all students, whether their answers are right or wrong, with the same query: "Tell me about your thinking." This consistent reply to every student's response signifies an important belief about her role as a teacher. Her goal is not to correct a student's idea but to figure out how what the student has done makes sense to him or her so that Mrs. Chen-Wu can make pedagogical decisions (in the next question or task posed) that build from the student's understanding.

A primary goal of Sra. Jones's use of questioning as a pedagogical tool is to bring students' thinking to the table. Posing follow-up questions after initial student responses provides space for students to explain their thinking and encourages all students to reflect on their stance toward the responses and to challenge or add on to those ideas. Learning mathematics is driven by the students' dialogue and relies very little on the teacher explicitly giving knowledge to students.

Mrs. Orozco and her colleagues connected parents' lived experiences with using mathematics with how students are expected to engage in mathematics in the classroom. Parents participated in meaningful mathematics investigations with their children. Teaching toward the understanding of powerful mathematics requires work beyond the classroom walls and has more impact when students, teachers, site leadership, families, and district administrators share a common vision. It is important that teachers also view parents as sense makers in this work.

Principle 3: Nurture a mathematics community of learners.

Student contributions permeate all three teaching episodes. The voices heard most in the vignettes are those of the students. This is not to imply a lesser role for teachers. In fact, the teachers, though not in the forefront, play a critical role in deciding on the nature of the task, guiding the discussions, and eliciting and building on multiple forms of student contributions to establish a social culture of collaborative learning. It is the teachers' expert knowledge of both mathematics and mathematics pedagogy that allows them to purposefully guide students' learning.

Note how Mrs. Chen-Wu draws students' attention to the thinking of their peers: "Listen closely to your partner; I may call on you to explain your partner's thinking." This is an intentional move to orient students to one another. Mrs. Chen-Wu has noted that she has a handful of students who frequently raise their hands to share, but their ideas do not always build on those of their classmates. She uses strategies to help students learn to better attend to one another's ideas and to encourage more students to take risks in sharing their thinking. In the example above, as a way to build competence, Mrs. Chen-Wu strategically highlights the thinking of a particular student who is still developing confidence in sharing with the rest of the class.

Orienting students to each other is at the heart of Sra. Jones's practice. Through collaborative work, a community of learners emerges. This community approach to learning prompts students to see each other as resources. Moreover, students come to expect that they will learn more and become stronger mathematicians through their collaborative work. Students develop skills in constructing viable arguments and have greater perseverance in sticking with problems. As Lilia, one of her students, states, "We get to share our ideas with everyone. That helps because then people can add on to your ideas to make it easier for me to get it."

For Mrs. Orozco, a community of mathematics learners includes more than just students. Teachers are learners as they become more proficient at listening to their students' mathematical ideas and responding with next steps. Parents are learners as they engage with schools to learn shifts needed for their children to be successful with new mathematics standards. Children can be powerful learners as they authentically engage in tasks that gently challenge them to extend their thinking. Parent engagement efforts require facilitators to be learners, as they plan, deliver, and debrief sessions. This requires learning about the families and communities students come from and collaborating across boundaries of classroom, grade, and culture to create opportunities to come together as a community to learn about mathematics and about one another.

Authors' Final Reflections

We began writing this book with the premise that understanding is the most fundamental goal of mathematics instruction. We then asked ourselves: "What are the characteristics of learning environments in which students successfully develop understanding of powerful mathematics by collaboratively building from their own reasoning and sense making and in ways that reflect and respect students' identities and communities?" Our goal throughout this book has been to provide the most complete and useful answer possible to this question. We used two methods: The first was to examine each dimension of the learning environment (Chapters 1–5) and what research and theory could tell us about its role in supporting powerful mathematics learning. The second was to bring each dimension to life through concrete examples and artifacts to provide a glimpse of how these features play out for real teachers and real students in real classrooms. Then, in this last chapter, we presented episodes from three schools to illustrate how the five dimensions of the learning environment are intertwined and work together to support success for all students. Rather than a series of discrete components, their benefits come from how these dimensions function together as a coherent, integrated system that promotes and sustains a productive learning environment for mathematics learning.

A diverse array of teachers, students, families, and communities were featured throughout the book to make it clear that a rich mathematics learning environment is possible to create in any school but does not have to look the same across every school. It is not prescribed and does not consist of a step-by-step method of instruction but rather reflects a tightly connected set of principles grounded in three core beliefs:

1. Instruction must focus on teaching mathematics for understanding.

2. Students are sense makers, and instruction must build on students' existing knowledge.

3. A community approach to learning mathematics advances and deepens everyone's learning—that of the teacher, the students, and the families.

We hope that this book provides opportunities for you to reflect individually and collectively on the type of learning environment that best supports your students' growth, and your own growth, as learners of mathematics. Indeed, one of the privileges of being a teacher is the opportunity to always learn. May the resources in this book serve to support your continued reflection and learning as much as putting them together has helped us to learn and grow in the work we do.

Appendix A:

Tools and Technology at a Glance

This table lists the name and type of tools and technology featured in the book. In addition to providing an easy way to find this resource, the table separates the tools and technology by their instructional purpose: making sense of mathematics, promoting collaboration, and eliciting and using evidence of student thinking. Remember, teachers must judiciously adopt technology and tools for their value in enhancing mathematics instruction, not simply for the sake of using them.

Tool or Technology	Instructional Purpose	Page
Chapter 1: The Physical and Virtual Environment		
Digital learning spaces	Promoting collaboration; eliciting and using evidence of student thinking Digital platforms as extended learning spaces	
Tool selection	Promoting mathematical reasoning and sense making Teacher strategy to encourage students' judicious selection of manipulatives during math investigations	
Chapter 2: The Discourse-Rich Environment		
Mathematics visualization software	Promoting mathematical reasoning and sense making Virtual manipulatives to assist in visualizing mathematical relationships and to support reasoning and problem solving	

Screencasting apps	Promoting mathematical reasoning and sense making; promoting collaboration	
	Screencasting as a vehicle for students to share and examine their own and their peers' thinking and mathematical reasoning	
Quick response (QR) code (video clip)	Promoting mathematical reasoning and sense making	
	A class use of QR codes to move classroom mathematics beyond the answer	

Chapter 3: The Task-Rich Environment

Quick images	Promoting mathematical reasoning and sense making	
	Visualizing number combinations to promote relational thinking	
Conceptual flashcards	Promoting mathematical reasoning and sense making	
	Flashcards incorporating visual models to support mastery of addition, subtraction, and multiplication facts	

Chapter 4: The Assessment-Rich Environment

Screencasting apps	Eliciting and using evidence of student thinking	
	The use of digital platforms to store photos of student work or videos of student problem solving for later discussion.	
Student response system	Eliciting and using evidence of student thinking	
	Digital student response systems to monitor student progress and provide feedback	
Base-ten blocks, coins, and hundredths grid	Promoting mathematical reasoning and sense making	
	Multiple representations of decimal numbers (specifically tenths and hundredths) to support students in revising and refining their understanding of decimal place values	
Digital classroom and student response system	Eliciting and using evidence of student thinking	
	Virtual sites to upload assignments and view students' work in real time	

Chapter 5: Extending the Classroom: Families and Communities

Web-based media sharing	Promoting collaboration with families and communities	
	Web-based platforms to share video recordings of classroom mathematics teaching practices with students' families	

Videoconferencing	Promoting collaboration Web-based audio and video calling apps to allow teachers to meet remotely with students and families	
Classroom websites	Promoting collaboration Class website to provide for information sharing and as a bidirectional communication tool	

Chapter 6: Moving from Vision to Reality: Bringing the Elements Together

Video-recorded interviews	Promoting collaboration; promoting mathematical reasoning and sense making The use of video-recorded interviews to examine students'/parents' application of mathematics in their everyday lives	

Appendix B:

Accompanying Materials at More4U

Chapter 1: The Physical and Virtual Environment

- Odd and Even Assignment (student handout)
- Math Wall Lesson (video clip)
- Strategies for Your Classroom: Considerations for Designing Your Physical Environment (teacher resource)

Chapter 2: The Discourse-Rich Environment

- Ms. Lawyer's Math Talk Vignette (transcript)
- Student Dictionary Template (student handout)
- Talk Moves to Support Discourse (teacher resource)
- Color-Coding Group Work Example (poster)
- Collaborative Group Responsibilities (student handout)
- Discourse Norms (teacher resource)
- Conversational Prompts (student handout)
- Mrs. Freedman-Finch's Task Launch (video clip)
- Discussing Group Discussion Norms (video clip)
- Purposeful Questions (teacher resource)
- Strategies for Your Classroom: Considerations for Designing and Sustaining a Discourse-Rich Environment (teacher resource)

Chapter 3: The Task-Rich Environment

- Cognitive Demand and Features of Task (teacher resource)
- Problem-Solving Sheets (2) (student handouts)
- Quilt Problem (PowerPoint)
- Mrs. Freedman-Finch's Bet Line Strategy (video clip)
- Clock Buddies Template (student handout)
- Kindergarten Student Explaining Reasoning Using Educreation (video clip)
- Quilt Problem Classroom Discussions (2 video clips)
- Strategies for Your Classroom: Considerations for Designing a Task-Rich Environment (teacher resource)

Chapter 4: The Assessment-Rich Environment

- Bilingual Decimal Place-Value Chart (student handout)
- Decimals Card Sort (student handout)
- Card Sort Template (teacher resource)
- Students Sharing Their Decimal Card Sort (2 video clips)
- Correct and Incorrect Sheet (student handout)
- True or False and Why Sheet (student handout)
- Mathematical Practices Recording Chart (teacher and student resource)
- Caught in the Act Citation (teacher resource)
- MP Self-Reflection Tool (student handout)
- My Math Learning Goals for the Year (student handout)
- Strategies for Your Classroom: Considerations for Designing an Assessment-Rich Environment (teacher resource)

Chapter 5: Extending the Classroom: Families and Communities

- Ms. Malpass Takes Attendance (video clip)
- Personal Numbers Assignment (student assignment)
- Home Visit Letter Template (teacher resource)
- Phone Call Home Script (teacher resource)
- Packaging Task (PowerPoint)

- Blank Squares (student handouts)
- Strategies for Your Classroom and School: Considerations for Promoting Family Engagement (teacher resource)

Chapter 6: Moving from Vision to Reality: Bringing the Elements Together

- Attendance Double Ten-Frame (teacher resource)
- How Do You Use Math Every Day? (2 video clips)
- Family Math Night Handout (teacher resource)
- Mrs. Orozco's Family Math Night Discussion (video clip)
- Family Engagement Session Closure (video clip)

References

Aguirre, Julia, Karen Mayfield-Ingram, and Danny Bernard Martin. *The Impact of Identity in K–8 Mathematics Learning and Teaching: Rethinking Equity-Based Practices.* Reston, Va.: National Council of Teachers of Mathematics, 2013.

Anderson, Lorin W., and David R. Krathwohl, eds. *A Taxonomy for Learning, Teaching, and Assessing: A Revision of Bloom's Taxonomy of Educational Objectives.* Boston: Allyn & Bacon, 2001.

Arndt, Petra A. "Design of Learning Spaces: Emotional and Cognitive Effects of Learning Environments in Relation to Child Development." *Mind, Brain, and Education* 6, no. 1 (2012): 41–48.

Ashlock, Robert B. *Error Patterns in Computation: Using Error Patterns to Help Each Student Learn.* 10th ed. Boston: Allyn & Bacon, 2009.

Barnard, Wendy M. "Parent Involvement in Elementary School and Educational Attainment." *Children and Youth Services Review* 26, no. 1 (2004): 39–62.

Bartel, V. B. "Home and School Factors Impacting Parental Involvement in a Title I Elementary School." *Journal of Research in Childhood Education* 24, no. 3 (2010): 209–28.

Bay-Williams, Jennifer M., and Gina Kling. "Enriching Addition and Subtraction Fact Mastery through Games." *Teaching Children Mathematics* 21, no. 4 (2014): 238–47.

Berry, Robert Q. III, and Mark W. Ellis. "Multidimensional Teaching." Mathematics Teaching in the Middle School 19, no. 3 (2013): 172–78.

Black, Paul, and Dylan Wiliam. "Assessment and Classroom Learning." *Assessment in Education: Principles, Policy & Practice* 5, no. 1 (1998): 7–74.

Boaler, Jo. *Experiencing School Mathematics: Teaching Styles, Sex, and Setting.* Buckingham, UK: Open University Press, 1997.

_____. *What's Math Got to Do with It?* New York: Penguin Books, 2008.

_____. *Mathematical Mindsets.* San Francisco, Calif.: Jossey-Bass, 2015.

Boaler, Jo, and Megan Staples. "Creating Mathematical Futures through an Equitable Teaching Approach: The Case of Railside School." *Teachers College Record* 110, no. 3 (2008): 608–45.

Boaler, Jo, Cathy Williams, and Amanda Confer. "Fluency without Fear: Research Evidence on the Best Ways to Learn Math Facts." YouCubed. January 28, 2015. http://www .youcubed.org/fluency-without-fear/

Bransford, John D., Ann L. Brown, and Rodney R. Cocking, eds. *How People Learn: Brain, Mind, Experience, and School.* Expanded ed. National Research Council Committee on Developments in the Science of Learning and Committee on Learning Research and Educational Practice. Washington, D.C.: National Academy Press, 2000.

Bray, Wendy. "Picture It: Flashcards That Encourage Reasoning." *Teaching Children Mathematics* 20, no. 6 (2014): 400.

Brenner, Mary E. "Adding Cognition to the Formula for Culturally Relevant Instruction in Mathematics." *Anthropology & Education Quarterly* 29, no. 2 (1998): 214–44.

Brownell, W. A. "Psychological Considerations in the Learning and Teaching of Arithmetic." In *The Teaching of Arithmetic.* 10th Yearbook of the National Council of Teachers of Mathematics, edited by W. D. Reeve, pp. 1–33. New York: Teachers College Press, 1935.

California Department of Education (CDE). *Mathematics Framework for California Public Schools.* Sacramento, Calif.: CDE, 2015.

Carpenter, Thomas P. "Learning to Add and Subtract: An Exercise in Problem Solving." In *Teaching and Learning Mathematical Problem Solving: Multiple Research Perspectives,* edited by Edward A. Silver. Hillsdale, N.J.: Lawrence Erlbaum Associates, 1985.

Carpenter, Thomas P., Elizabeth Fennema, Penelope L. Peterson, Chi-Pang Chiang, and Megan Loef. "Using Knowledge of Children's Mathematics Thinking in Classroom Teaching: An Experimental Study." *American Educational Research Journal* 26, no. 4 (1989): 499–531.

Carpenter, Thomas P., Megan Loef Franke, and Linda Levi. *Thinking Mathematically: Integrating Arithmetic and Algebra in Elementary Schools.* Portsmouth, N.H.: Heinemann, 2003.

Chapin, Suzanne H., Catherine O'Connor, and Nancy Canavan Anderson. *Classroom Discussions: Using Math Talk to Help Students Learn.* 2nd ed. Sausalito, Calif.: Math Solutions, 2009.

Charles, Randall I. "Big Ideas and Understandings as the Foundation for Elementary and Middle School Mathematics." *Journal of Mathematics Education Leadership* 7, no. 3 (2005): 9–24.

Cheryan, Sapna, Sianna A. Ziegler, Victoria C. Plaut, and Andrew N. Meltzoff. "Designing Classrooms to Maximize Student Achievement." *Policy Insights from the Behavioral and Brain Sciences* 1, no. 1 (2014): 4–12.

Civil, Marta, and Rosi Andrade. "Transitions between Home and School Mathematics: Rays of Hope amidst the Passing Clouds." In *Transitions between Contexts of Mathematical Practices,* edited by Guida de Abreu, Alan J. Bishop, and Norma C. Presmeg, pp. 149–69. Dordrecht, The Netherlands: Kluwer, 2002.

Clements. Douglas H., and Julie Sarama. "Standards for Preschoolers." *Teaching Children Mathematics* 7, no. 1 (2000): 38–41.

Cohen, Elizabeth, G., Rachel A. Lotan, Beth A. Scarloss, and Adele R. Arellano. "Complex Instruction: Equity in Cooperative Learning Classrooms." *Theory into Practice* 38, no. 2 (1999): 80–86.

Darling-Hammond, Linda, Edward Haertel, and James Pellegrino. "Making Good Use of New Assessments: Interpreting and Using Scores from the Smarter Balanced Assessment Consortium." Smarter Balanced Assessment Consortium, March 2015. http://education.vermont.gov/documents/EDU-WhitePaper-Making_Good_Use-of_New_Assessments.pdf

Dick, Lara, Tracy Foote White, Aaron Trocki, Paola Sztajn, Daniel Heck, and Kate Herrema. "Supporting Sense Making with Mathematical Bet Lines." *Teaching Children Mathematics* 22, no. 9 (2016): 538–45.

Drake, Corey, Tonia J. Land, Tonya Gau Bartell, Julia M. Aguirre, Mary Q. Foote, Amy Roth McDuffie, and Erin E. Turner. "Three Strategies for Opening Curriculum Spaces: Building on Children's Multiple Mathematical Knowledge Bases While Using Curriculum Materials." *Teaching Children Mathematics* 21, no. 6 (2015): 346–52.

Durkin, Kelley, and Bethany Rittle-Johnson. "Diagnosing Misconceptions: Revealing Changing Decimal Fraction Knowledge." *Learning and Instruction* 37 (2015): 21–29.

Durkin, Kelley, and Bethany Rittle-Johnson. "The Effectiveness of Using Incorrect Examples to Support Learning about Decimal Magnitude." *Learning and Instruction* 22, no. 3 (2012): 206–14.

Engle, Randi A., and Faith R. Conant. "Guiding Principles for Fostering Productive Disciplinary Engagement: Explaining an Emergent Argument in a Community of Learners Classroom." *Cognition and Instruction* 20, no. 4 (2002): 399–483.

Ernest, Paul. "Forms of Knowledge in Mathematics and Mathematics Education: Philosophical and Rhetorical Perspectives." In *Forms of Mathematical Knowledge: Learning and Teaching with Understanding*, edited by Dina Tirosh. Dordrecht, The Netherlands: Kluwer, 1999.

Esmonde, Indigo. "Ideas and identities: Supporting Equity in Cooperative Mathematics Learning." *Review of Educational Research* 79, no. 2 (2009): 1008–43.

Ferlazzo, Larry. "Involvement or Engagement?" *Educational Leadership* 68, no. 8 (2011): 10–14.

Ferlazzo, Larry, and Lorie Hammond. *Building Parent Engagement in Schools.* Santa Barbara, Calif.: Linworth, 2009.

Foote, Mary Q. "Crossing the Border between Home and School: Dominican Parents' Perspectives on the Teaching and Learning of Mathematics." In *Transnational and Borderland Studies in Mathematics Education*, edited by Richard S. Kitchen and Marta Civil, pp. 23–45. New York: Routledge, 2011.

González, Norma, Luis C. Moll, and Cathy Amanti, eds. *Funds of Knowledge: Theorizing Practices in Households, Communities, and Classrooms.* London: Routledge, 2005.

Goodall, Janet, and Caroline Montgomery. "Parental Involvement to Parental Engagement: A Continuum." *Educational Review* 66, no. 4 (2014): 399–410.

Gutiérrez, Kris D., and Barbara Rogoff. "Cultural Ways of Learning: Individual Traits or Repertoires of Practice." *Educational Researcher* 32, no. 5 (2003): 19–25.

Gutstein, Eric. "Teaching and Learning Mathematics for Social Justice in an Urban, Latino School." *Journal for Research in Mathematics Education* 34, no. 1 (2003): 37–73.

Hattie, John. *Visible Learning for Teachers: Maximizing Impact on Learning.* New York: Routledge, 2012.

Henderson, Anne T., and Karen A. Mapp. *A New Wave of Evidence: The Impact of School, Family, and Community Connections on Student Achievement.* Austin, Tex.: Southwest Educational Development Laboratory, 2002.

Henningsen, Marjorie, and Mary Kay Stein. "Mathematical Tasks and Student Cognition: Classroom-Based Factors That Support and Inhibit High-Level Mathematical Thinking and Reasoning." *Journal for Research in Mathematics Education* 28, no. 5 (1997): 524–49.

Hiebert, James, ed. *Conceptual and Procedural Knowledge: The Case of Mathematics.* Hillsdale, N.J.: Lawrence Erlbaum Associates, 1986.

Hiebert, James, and Thomas P. Carpenter. "Learning and Teaching with Understanding." In *Handbook of Research on Mathematics Teaching and Learning*, edited by Douglas A. Grouws, pp. 65–97. New York: Macmillan, 1992.

Hiebert, James, and Patricia Lefevre. "Conceptual and Procedural Knowledge in Mathematics: An Introductory Analysis." In *Conceptual and Procedural Knowledge: The Case of Mathematics*, edited by James Hiebert, pp. 1–27. Hillsdale, N.J.: Lawrence Erlbaum Associates, 1986.

Horn, Ilana S. "Fast Kids, Slow Kids, Lazy Kids: Framing the Mismatch Problem in Mathematics Teachers' Conversations." *Journal of the Learning Sciences* 16, no. 1 (2007): 37–79.

Jackson, Kara J., Emily C. Shahan, Lynsey K. Gibbons, and Paul A. Cobb. "Launching Complex Tasks." *Mathematics Teaching in the Middle School* 18, no. 1 (2012): 24–29.

Janes, Rita C., and Elizabeth L. Strong. *Numbers and Stories: Using Children's Literature to Teach Young Children Number Sense.* Thousand Oaks, Calif.: Corwin, 2014.

Jeynes, William H. "A Meta-Analysis of the Relation of Parent Involvement to Urban Elementary School Student Academic Achievement." *Urban Education* 40, no. 3 (2005): 237–69.

Kazemi, Elham, and Allison Hintz. *Intentional Talk: How to Structure and Lead Productive Mathematical Discussions.* Portland, Maine: Stenhouse Publishers, 2014.

King-Sears, Margaret. "Universal Design for Learning: Technology and Pedagogy." *Learning Disability Quarterly* 32, no. 4 (2009): 199–201.

Kisker, Ellen Eliason, Jerry Lipka, Barbara L. Adams, Anthony Rickard, Dora Andrew-Ihrke, Eva Evelyn Yanez, and Ann Millard. "The Potential of a Culturally Based Supplemental Mathematics Curriculum to Improve the Mathematics Performance of Alaska Native and Other Students." *Journal for Research in Mathematics Education* 43, no. 1 (2012): 75–113.

Kling, Gina, and Jennifer M. Bay-Williams. "Assessing Basic Fact Fluency." *Teaching Children Mathematics* 20, no. 8 (2014): 488–97.

Land, Tonia J., Corey Drake, Molly Sweeney, Natalie Franke, and Jennifer M. Johnson. *Transforming the Task with Number Choice: Kindergarten through Grade 3.* Reston, Va.: National Council of Teachers of Mathematics, 2015.

Lareau, Annette. *Unequal Childhoods: Class, Race, and Family Life.* Berkeley, Calif.: University of California Press, 2003.

Lee, Jaekyung. "College for All: Gaps between Desirable and Actual P–12 Math Achievement Trajectories for College Readiness." *Educational Researcher* 41, no. 2 (2012): 43–55.

Lehrer, Richard, and Lee Shumow. "Aligning the Construction Zones of Parents and Teachers for Mathematics Reform." *Cognition and Instruction* 15, no. 1 (1997): 41–83.

Lubienski, Sarah Theule. "Traditional or Standards-Based Mathematics? The Choices of Students and Parents in One District." *Journal of Curriculum and Supervision* 19, no. 4 (2004): 338–65.

Ma, Liping. *Knowing and Teaching Elementary Mathematics: Teachers' Understanding of Fundamental Mathematics in China and the United States.* Mahwah, N.J.: Lawrence Erlbaum Associates, 1999.

Martin, Danny B. "Mathematics Learning and Participation as Racialized Forms of Experience: African American Parents Speak on the Struggle for Mathematics Literacy." *Mathematical Thinking and Learning* 8, no. 3 (2006): 197–229.

Martin, Sandra Horne. "The Classroom Environment and Its Effects on the Practice of Teachers." *Journal of Environmental Psychology* 22, nos. 1–2 (2002): 139–56.

Marx, Alexandra, Urs Fuhrer, and Terry Hartig. "Effects of Classroom Seating Arrangements on Children's Question-Asking." *Learning Environments Research* 2, no. 3 (1999): 249–63.

McGregor, Jane. "Space, Power and the Classroom." *Forum* 46, no. 1 (2004): 13–18.

Michaels, Sarah, Catherine O'Connor, and Lauren B. Resnick. "Deliberative Discourse Idealized and Realized: Accountable Talk in the Classroom and in Civic Life." *Studies in Philosophy and Education* 27, no. 4 (2008): 283–97.

Middleton, James, and Amanda Jansen. *Motivation Matters and Interest Counts: Fostering Engagement in Mathematics*. Reston, Va.: National Council of Teachers of Mathematics, 2011.

Moll, Luis C., and Norma González. "Teachers as Social Scientists: Learning about Culture from Household Research." In *Race, Ethnicity, and Multiculturalism: Policy and Practice Vol. 1*, edited by Peter Hall, pp. 89–114. Hamden, Conn.: Garland Publishing, 1997.

Moschkovich, Judit N. "Understanding the Needs of Latino Students in Reform-Oriented Mathematics Classrooms." In *Changing the Faces of Mathematics: Perspectives on Latinos*, edited by Luis Ortiz-Franco, Norma G. Hernandez, and Yolanda de la Cruz, pp. 5–12. Reston, Va.: National Council of Teachers of Mathematics, 1999.

Moses, Robert P., and Charles E. Cobb Jr. *Radical Equations: Math Literacy and Civil Rights*. Boston: Beacon Press, 2001.

Moyer, Patricia S., and M. Gail Jones. "Controlling Choice: Teachers, Students, and Manipulatives in Mathematics Classrooms." *School Science and Mathematics* 104, no. 1 (2004): 16–31.

Mullis, Ina V. S., Michael O. Martin, Pierre Foy, and Alka Arora. *TIMSS 2011 International Results in Mathematics*. Chestnut Hill, Mass.: TIMSS & PIRLS International Study Center, Lynch School of Education, Boston College, 2012.

National Council of Teachers of Mathematics (NCTM). *Principles and Standards for School Mathematics*. Reston, Va.: NCTM, 2000.

_____. *Principles to Actions: Ensuring Mathematical Success for All*. Reston, Va.: NCTM, 2014a.

_____. "Procedural Fluency in Mathematics." Reston, Va.: NCTM, 2014b. http://www
.nctm.org/Standards-and-Positions/Position-Statements/Procedural-Fluency-in
-Mathematics/

National Education Association. "Research Spotlight on Academic Ability Grouping: NEA Reviews of the Research on Best Practices in Education." Retrieved February 16, 2015, from http://www.nea.org/tools/16899.htm

National Governors Association Center for Best Practices and Council of Chief State School Officers (NGA Center and CCSSO). *Common Core State Standards for Mathematics*. Washington, D.C.: NGA Center and CCSSO, 2010. http://www.corestandards.org

National Research Council. *Adding It Up: Helping Children Learn Mathematics*. Mathematics Learning Study Committee. Jeremy Kilpatrick, Jane Swafford, and Bradford Findell, eds. Center for Education, Division of Behavioral and Social Sciences and Education. Washington, D.C.: National Academy Press, 2001.

_____. *National Science Education Standards*. Washington, D.C.: National Academy Press, 1996.

Patrikakou, Evanthia N. *The Power of Parent Involvement: Evidence, Ideas, and Tools for Student Success.* Lincoln, Ill.: Center on Innovation & Improvement, 2008.

Planas, Núria, and Marta Civil. "Language-as-Resource and Language-as-Political: Tensions in the Bilingual Mathematics Classroom." *Mathematics Education Research Journal* 25, no. 3 (2013): 361–78.

Pomerantz, Eva M., Elizabeth A. Moorman, and Scott D. Litwack. "The How, Whom, and Why of Parents' Involvement in Children's Academic Lives: More Is Not Always Better." *Review of Educational Research* 77, no. 3 (2007): 373–410.

Poza, Luis, Maneka Deanna Brooks, and Guadalupe Valdés. "'Entre Familia': Immigrant Parents' Strategies for Involvement in Children's Schooling." *School Community Journal* 24, no. 1 (2014): 119–48.

Pritchard, Robert, Susan O'Hara, and Jeff Zwiers. "Using New Technologies to Engage and Support English Language Learners in Mathematics Classrooms." In *Cases on Technology Integration in Mathematics Education,* edited by Drew Polly, pp. 144–61. Hershey, Pa.: Information Science Reference, 2014.

Project Tomorrow. *The New 3 E's of Education: Enabled, Engaged, Empowered. How Today's Students Are Leveraging Emerging Technologies for Learning.* Irvine, Calif.: Project Tomorrow, 2011. http://www.tomorrow.org/speakup/pdfs/SU10_3EofEducation(Students).pdf

Razfar, Aria, Lena Licón Khisty, and Kathryn Chval. "Re-Mediating Second Language Acquisition: A Sociocultural Perspective for Language Development." *Mind, Culture, and Activity* 18, no. 3 (2011): 195–215.

Ribble, Mike. "Digital Citizenship for Educational Change." *Kappa Delta Pi Record* 48, no. 4 (2012): 148–51.

Rittle-Johnson, Bethany, Michael Schneider, and Jon Star. "Not a One-Way Street: Bidirectional Relations between Procedural and Conceptual Knowledge of Mathematics." *Educational Psychology Review* 27, no. 4 (2015): 587–97.

Roschelle, Jeremy, Ken Rafanan, Ruchi Bhanot, Gucci Estrella, Bill Penuel, Miguel Nussbaum, and Susana Claro. "Scaffolding Group Explanation and Feedback with Handheld Technology: Impact on Students' Mathematics Learning." *Educational Technology Research and Development* 58, no. 4 (2010): 399–419.

Rothstein, Richard. "How to Fix Our Schools: It's More Complicated, and More Work, Than the Klein-Rhee 'Manifesto' Wants You to Believe" (Issue Brief 286). Washington, D.C.: Economic Policy Institute, October 14, 2010.

Sarama, Julie, and Douglas H. Clements. "'Concrete' Computer Manipulatives in Mathematics Education." *Child Development Perspectives* 3, no. 3 (2009): 145–50.

Schoenfeld, Alan. H. "What's All the Fuss about Metacognition?" In *Cognitive Science and Mathematics Education,* edited by Alan H. Schoenfeld, pp. 189–215. Hillsdale, N.J.: Lawrence Erlbaum Associates, 1987.

Sheldon, Steven B., and Joyce L. Epstein. "Involvement Counts: Family and Community Partnerships and Mathematics Achievement." *Journal of Educational Research* 98, no. 4 (2005): 196–207.

Shumow, Lee. "Promoting Parental Attunement to Children's Mathematical Reasoning through Parent Education." *Journal of Applied Developmental Psychology* 19, no. 1 (1998): 109–27.

———. "The Task Matters: Parental Assistance to Children Doing Different Homework Assignments." *School Community Journal* 13, no. 2 (2003): 7–24.

Small, Marian. *Good Questions: Great Ways to Differentiate Mathematics Instruction.* Reston, Va.: National Council of Teachers of Mathematics, 2009.

Smith, John P., III, Andrea A. diSessa, and Jeremy Roschelle. "Misconceptions Reconceived: A Constructivist Analysis of Knowledge in Transition." *The Journal of the Learning Sciences* 3, no. 2 (1993–1994): pp. 115–63.

Smith, Margaret S., and Mary Kay Stein. *5 Practices for Orchestrating Productive Mathematics Discussions.* Reston, Va.: National Council of Teachers of Mathematics, 2011.

Stein, Mary Kay, Barbara W. Grover, and Marjorie Henningsen. "Building Student Capacity for Mathematical Thinking and Reasoning: An Analysis of Mathematical Tasks Used in Reform Classrooms." *American Educational Research Journal* 33, no. 2 (1996): 455–88.

Stein, Mary Kay, and Suzanne Lane. "Instructional Tasks and the Development of Student Capacity to Think and Reason: An Analysis of the Relationship between Teaching and Learning in a Reform Mathematics Project." *Educational Research and Evaluation: An International Journal on Theory and Practice* 2, no. 1 (1996): 50–80.

Stein, Mary Kay, Janine Remillard, and Margaret Smith. "How Curriculum Influences Student Learning." In *Second Handbook of Research on Mathematics Teaching and Learning,* edited by Frank K. Lester, Jr., pp. 319–69. Reston, Va.: National Council of Teachers of Mathematics, 2007.

Stein, Mary Kay, Margaret Schwan Smith, Marjorie Henningsen, and Edward A. Silver. *Implementing Standards-Based Mathematics Instruction: A Casebook for Professional Development.* 2nd ed. New York: Teachers College Press; Reston, Va.: National Council of Teachers of Mathematics, 2009.

Suh, Jennifer, and Patricia S. Moyer. "Developing Students' Representational Fluency Using Virtual and Physical Algebra Balances." *Journal of Computers in Mathematics and Science Teaching* 26, no. 2 (2007): 155–73.

U.S. Department of Education. "National Assessment of Educational Progress (NAEP) Mathematics Scale Score of 8th-Graders with Various Attitudes toward Mathematics and Percentage Reporting These Attitudes, by Selected Student Characteristics: 2013." U.S. Department of Education, Oct. 23, 2014.

U.S. Department of Education, National Center for Education Statistics (NCES). *Teaching Mathematics in Seven Countries: Results from the TIMSS 1999 Video Study* (NCES 2003–013 Revised). Washington, D.C.: U.S. Department of Education, 2003.

Van de Walle, John A., Karen S. Karp, and Jennifer M. Bay-Williams. *Elementary and Middle School Mathematics: Teaching Developmentally.* 7th ed. New York: Pearson, 2009.

Van Voorhis, Frances L. "Adding Families to the Homework Equation: A Longitudinal Study of Mathematics Achievement." *Education and Urban Society* 43, no. 3 (2011): 313–38.

Webb, Noreen M., Megan L. Franke, Marsha Ing, Jacqueline Wong, Cecilia H. Fernandez, Nami Shin, and Angela C. Turrou. "Engaging with Others' Mathematical Ideas: Interrelationships among Student Participation, Teachers' Instructional Practices, and Learning." *International Journal of Educational Research* 63 (2014): 79–93.

Webb, Norman L. "Criteria for Alignment of Expectations and Assessments in Mathematics and Science Education." Research Monograph No. 8. National Institute for Science Education. Washington D.C.: Council of Chief State School Officers, 1997.

Weiss, Heather B., Suzanne M. Bouffard, Beatrice L. Bridglall, and Edmund W. Gordon. "Reframing Family Involvement in Education: Supporting Families to Support Educational Equity." *Equity Matters. Research Review No. 5.* A Research Initiative of the Campaign for Educational Equity, Teachers College, Columbia University (2009).

Weissglass, Julian. "Inequity in Mathematics Education: Questions for Educators." *Mathematics Educator* 12, no. 2 (2002): 34–39.

Wiliam, Dylan. *Embedded Formative Assessment.* Bloomington, Ind.: Solution Tree Press, 2011.

Yeh, Cathery. "Worth a Thousand Words." *Teaching Children Mathematics* 21, no. 8 (2015): 512.

About the Authors

Cathery Yeh is an assistant professor in the College of Educational Studies at Chapman University. Her professional work experience spans sixteen years, beginning with her tenure as an elementary school teacher and teacher educator to serving the mathematics education community as an author, editor, and editorial panel member for NCTM's journal, *Teaching Children Mathematics*, and as a professional development facilitator and mathematics task writer with Illustrative Mathematics. Cathery can usually be found in her favorite place—mathematics classrooms—working and learning with students and teachers.

Mark W. Ellis is a professor of education at California State University, Fullerton. He served on the National Council of Teachers of Mathematics (NCTM) Board of Directors from 2011–2014 and contributed to the development of NCTM's *Principles to Action: Ensuring Mathematical Success for All.* Prior to entering higher education, Mark taught mathematics in grades 6–12 in northern California public schools for six years, earning National Board certification in early adolescence mathematics in 1999. All of his work is driven by a belief that every student has the potential to be successful in learning mathematics and a commitment to ensuring this potential is fulfilled in every classroom.

Carolee Koehn Hurtado, a former high school mathematics teacher, serves as the Director of the UCLA Mathematics Project and UCLA Parent Project at Center X in the UCLA Graduate School of Education and Information Studies. Under her leadership and guidance, the Mathematics Project and Parent Project teams design and facilitate university-based, school-based, and district-based professional development. These opportunities empower parents and educators to form partnerships to provide an engaging and humanizing mathematical education for children with an explicit focus on equity and academic development.